I0796210

perch

Justin Champagne-Lagarde

photography by
Sarah Farmer

foreword by
Mandel Hitzer

perch

soil / land / sea

a cookbook

Figure.1
Vancouver / Toronto / Berkeley

Recipe Notes

We encourage you to use local ingredients.

Cocktail recipes are for one serving;
food recipes are for six.

Produce is always fresh and medium-sized.

Unless otherwise stated:

- Milk is whole.
- Sugar is white.
- Salt is kosher.

At the restaurant, we use:

- An Ankarsrum food mixer, but a stand mixer fitted with the appropriate attachment may be used instead.
- Binchotan charcoals with our Konro grill.
- Superflex by Martellato reusable piping bags.
- Smoked and flake salts from Vancouver Island Sea Salt. We also use their salts in all ferments.

We strongly recommend that when using a pressure cooker to cook meat, you naturally release the pressure, as opposed to force releasing.

Recipes are chef tested.

25 26 27 28 29 5 4 3 2 1

Cataloguing data is available from Library and Archives Canada
ISBN 978-1-77327-247-4 (hbk.)

Design by Naomi MacDougall | DSGN Dept.

Food and prop styling by Justin Champagne-Lagarde

Editing by Michelle Meade

Copy editing by Marnie Lamb

Proofreading by Christine Rowlands

Indexing by Iva Cheung

Printed and bound in China by Shenzhen Reliance Printing Co., Ltd.

Figure 1 Publishing Inc.
Vancouver BC Canada
www.figure1publishing.com

Figure 1 Publishing is located in the traditional, unceded territory of the xʷməθkʷəy̓əm (Musqueam), Sḵwx̱wú7mesh (Squamish), and səlilwətaɬ (Tsleil-Waututh) peoples.

To Amanda MacIntosh, this book was made possible because of you.

Contents

民

Foreword

Mandel Hitzer
chef and owner, deer + almond

I've long believed that food has the power to create community—to bring people together around a shared table where the stories that nourish us most are those we tell each other. Over the years, I've pursued that belief with passion at my own restaurant, deer + almond, and through projects like RAW:almond, where we turn unexpected places into unforgettable dining destinations. In this book, *Perch*, Chef Justin Champagne-Lagarde does something equally magical: he bridges the gap between soil, land, sea and the plate, offering an experience that is both intimately local and boundlessly creative.

The first time I learned about Justin's approach, I was struck by how thoroughly he follows each ingredient back to its source. He's not just looking for fresh produce or ethical proteins—he's collecting and sharing stories of farmers, foragers and artisans who share his commitment to sustainability and respect for the earth. It's one thing to talk about nose-to-tail or root-to-stem cooking. It's another to live it every day as Justin does, turning "kitchen scraps" into new forms of beauty and finding creative ways to compost and give back to the land. With *Perch*, Justin and his team challenge all of us to question how we cook and why we cook, setting a vision for a better, more responsible table.

I recognize a kindred spirit in Justin's decision to let creativity guide him through the more challenging moments of running a small restaurant. From navigating construction hiccups to juggling rising costs and sourcing unique ingredients, he's carved out a path that is uniquely his own—equal parts bold vision, playful experimentation and a profound love of feeding people well. Too often, we in the industry fall into the habit of repeating the familiar. But Perch is built on rethinking tradition, from how a dish is plated to how each course flows into the next. His tasting menus are an homage to Canada's incredible natural variety, driven by the question, "What's growing right here, right now, and how can I make it shine?"

That sense of place, of being rooted, resonates with me deeply. In Winnipeg, we must often contend with extremes like icy winters and short summers. Like many places, we also have the innate challenge of gathering a diverse community around a common, shared experience. Yet time and again, I see how food rises to the occasion. It becomes a universal language that connects local farmers, passionate cooks and curious diners. Perch reminds me of the joy of taking a simple root vegetable or a piece of freshly foraged produce, then transforming it into a dish that honours everything that went into growing it: the soil, the sun, the farmer's early-morning labour. Every recipe in this book carries that same respect.

As you read through these pages, you'll find much more than instructions for replicating the restaurant's dishes. You'll discover an approach—one that invites you to view every ingredient and every technique as part of a continuum that links personal creativity with environmental stewardship. It's a balance that takes real dedication, and *Perch* generously shares the lessons Justin has learned along the way. He shows us that a truly elevated meal is also an honest one. One that celebrates where we come from and the people we share it with.

Take these recipes into your kitchen with an open mind and a sense of adventure. Experiment with the local flavours in your own backyard, or try a new fermentation technique that once seemed too intimidating. Above all, remember the spirit that makes Perch special: a genuine belief that we can honour this planet by cooking with gratitude and curiosity. That, in the end, is what brings us together and keeps us coming back for more.

Mandel Hitzer is the chef and owner of deer + almond in Winnipeg, Manitoba, which opened in 2012 and which has been recognized multiple times in Canada's 100 Best.

How Perch Came to Be

The story of Perch begins with a text message and continues to fractured ribs during renovations—not a path I'd suggest to anyone opening a restaurant. Opening my own place and following my own vision were always my goals, even before my start at culinary school. Most cooks will tell you their "end goal" is to open their own restaurants, which is incredibly difficult and a ton scary but very rewarding!

I'd had the idea of my own place percolating in my mind for years, refining the concept almost daily until the dream was fully realized. I was walking my dog, Lambic, one morning, probably to go get coffee somewhere. A friend who, at the time, owned a beautiful little restaurant on Preston Street sent me a text. It simply read, "Would you be interested in taking over my restaurant space?" They wanted to expand their restaurant at a larger location and needed someone to sublease the remaining two and a half years on the space.

I was instantly interested and discussed it with my partner, Amanda MacIntosh. Being the incredibly supportive person that she is, she told me to go for it. The long work was just about to begin.

Community, Not Capital

Opening a restaurant is an incredibly expensive project, and I was living on a cook's wages with the savings account to match. I had to find the money, so I reached out to so many people for insight into finding an investor. From this initial foray, I got some amazing contacts, great new friends and an incredible support group... but no investors. This also occurred during COVID, and understandably, people were reluctant to put money into a new restaurant. So, instead, I found an organization called Futurpreneur, which teamed up with Business Development Bank of Canada to secure loans of up to $60,000 for young professionals looking to start businesses. After a lengthy, tedious and time-consuming loan application process, I received an approval two months later and officially took over the tiny space at 300 Preston Street in the last week of September 2021.

When I was seeking investors, I contacted my friend Robin Duetta, who is a gem of a human, to find out if he knew of any potential leads. For years, Robin has done so much for the Ottawa community, organizing fundraisers annually for people in need and supporting our local chefs! In response to my request, he introduced me to someone who has become a great friend and a mentor in the restaurant business world. Sandra MacInnes has incredible knowledge about everything to do with opening a restaurant, having owned and managed some of the finest in the city. She supported me at every step leading to the opening of Perch and even found the best deals on equipment and dinnerware for me. Robin and Sandra were both integral to the creation of the restaurant, and Perch wouldn't be Perch without them.

Gray Jay, the former restaurant on Preston Street, did such a great renovation on the space when they moved in, so we were lucky to need only cosmetic changes for our renovation, which helped us save a ton of money! We started our renos in late September, ripping out bench seating and random storage units. And while Amanda and I were on the same game page (apparently, this is a "Justinism"), we had so many ideas but didn't know how to put our plan into action. So Amanda reached out to her friend Bridget Sullivan and her partner, Jon Thibert, for support. Bridget is a real estate agent with a keen eye for staging houses, and Jon is an HVAC technician and a jack of all trades who can fix, build or do whatever a project might need. They became two key players in the creation of Perch.

Bridget put the chaotic ideas Amanda and I had onto paper and presented them as a vision board of sorts, and from there, we were off to the races. We'd arrive at the restaurant early in the morning and stay late into the evening, doing everything ourselves and with help from friends. We ate so many Lili pies from the eponymous restaurant a few doors down from Perch that, even years later, I can taste them as I type the words.

Gray Jay's ceiling was made of foam slats glued to a foam drop-down ceiling and painted a dark blue.

The last thing we wanted was for people to walk in and think "oh, you copied Gray Jay," so we wanted to change that to establish our own identity. As the budget was so tight, we had no choice but to paint the ceiling. The foam was glued to foam, which meant we couldn't use rollers or brushes, because they'd be time consuming and cause too much damage. Luckily, my buddy Michel Miller is great at this kind of thing and has all the tools needed. I bought gallons of paint. He showed up in what can only be described as "Dexter"-inspired outerwear and spent six hours with his hands above his head, painting the entire ceiling in two to three coats.

We were forever grateful, and in exchange, I offered a night out at the bar with any top-shelf Scotch he wanted. We went out the following night.

Falling Down (Literally), Rising Up

Once, I was on my way home after a long day at the site, and I ordered a couple of pounds of wings from the local pub to bring home to Amanda. I hopped on a rental e-scooter outside the pub door with the aim of getting home faster to eat the wings sooner. About four minutes into the journey, with the two pounds of wings in one hand and scooter throttle in the other, I hit a pothole, went flying and landed chest first on the scooter's stem. I spent a minute or two gasping for air before I eventually came to. I hopped back on the scooter once I had my bearings and finished the short trip home. (FYI, despite the disaster, I didn't lose a single wing.)

I figured the pain would diminish after a few days and things would return to normal, but I was wrong. We were in the middle of renovations, and I couldn't get out of bed or even put on socks without help or tearing up. A CT scan revealed a lacerated liver and two fractured ribs. Thankfully, Amanda, who already had a lot on her plate, took on even more responsibility (and made it look effortless).

The plan had been to open Perch by the end of October, but because of minor setbacks and delays, that just didn't work out. On November 12, 2021, we opened our doors to the public, sold out two seatings and had a great time showing Ottawa what we had envisioned for so long!

Our Thought Process

Opening a restaurant is a massive undertaking, requiring countless hours of consideration for interior design, menu planning, food and cocktail development, staffing, suppliers and associated administrative work. Most of the time, my peers and members of the hospitality community recognize and appreciate this. However, there are also those who are less than supportive and underestimate the amount of blood, sweat and tears we pour into the business. It never ceases to surprise me when a patron walks into a restaurant, shop or any small business, for that matter, and assumes they've cracked the code to creating a successful business—the mindset behind that behaviour eludes me, actually.

Our thought process is constantly evolving, and an expression I make today might change slightly by the time of this book's publication. However, every change is propelled by our beliefs, our guests' experiences and our desire to help create a sustainable world.

Atmosphere

Amanda and I spoke extensively about the atmosphere we wanted for Perch. I was certain that the dining experience had to feel cozy, intimate and informal. I likened it to having a tasting menu dinner at a friend's swanky house—after all, this is how I like to go out and eat.

We tried doing a small à la carte bar menu when we opened, but we weren't getting enough walk-ins for it and our tasting menu dining began to take off. So we scrapped the bar food menu and offered the tasting menu exclusively throughout our 900-square-foot restaurant.

We listened to endless podcasts about opening a restaurant (shout-out to *Opening Soon*) and read various studies about restaurant dining and what people unconsciously enjoy and dislike about the atmosphere. We knew our tasting menu restaurant needed to have a lively vibe. I eliminated tablecloths and the formality of suits and ties and turned up the music louder than most would expect.

The table touches at a tasting menu restaurant can be a sign of refinement and extra care, but I often feel these touches interrupt the experience. At many fine-dining restaurants, staff will come and top up your water from a carafe that's already at your table. While I appreciate attentive service, it can be distracting and halt conversation at the table—especially since the Canadian in me will thank them every time! So to minimize the disruption of our guests' dining experiences at Perch, we made concerted efforts to top up water only when the waitstaff was already at the table.

We decided to keep the same cutlery for each course. Our space is tiny, and if we'd had to maneuver around guests to grab pieces of cutlery, then squish next to them minutes later to reset new ones, it would have been more of a nuisance than reusing the existing cutlery at the table. Furthermore, we have limited space to store dirty dishes during service, and cutlery from twenty-six guests for nine courses can take up a lot of room! And since we don't have a dedicated dishwasher position, we all contribute by doing dishes whenever we can except for the crazy busy days when my friend Dave Wright comes in to help. (Thanks, Dave!)

Bar Program

This was a big conversation item during the early stages of the restaurant. Because our aim was to be a restaurant driven by Canadian products, we had to ask ourselves a lot of hard questions. Was it okay to bring in wines and spirits from other countries? What about citrus? Were garnishes too wasteful? To be honest, I don't know if we made all the right choices for the long term. We also strive for better, and the restaurant is forever evolving.

In the end, we concluded that we will always try to showcase Canadian spirits or wine (and always beer) where possible. However, spirits and wine from other countries are unavoidable mostly because of the archaic Canadian liquor laws, which result in the limited availability of some spirits and wine within Ontario, and we have to ensure that our portfolio is wide enough to make the beverage pairing interesting. We've introduced sake at the restaurant, sharing its amazing diversity and flavours with our guests. In fact, a unique sake on our pairing menu is the best way of showcasing the product to our guests.

To reduce waste, we decided to cut citrus unless we're able to get our hands on the beautiful O'Citrus from Quebec (page 155). For most bartenders, this would be like cutting off a limb—and understandably so. A whisky sour without lemon or a margarita without lime doesn't make sense. But citrus is such a wasteful ingredient and rarely fully used (whether by the bartender or the guest when used as a garnish). It also is typically shipped from thousands of kilometres away and rarely ever Canadian. (I'm aware of only two farms that grow citrus in Canada and can also handle restaurant sales.)

Not using citrus might seem impossible until you taste verjus, which is the juice from unripe grapes that wineries remove from the vines early in the season to help the other grapes grow and intensify. Canadian verjus all have their own flavour profiles, which add beautiful acidity to cocktails. While these flavours may not be perfect replicas of lemon or lime, they are delicious and bring a unique character to even classic cocktails. We also make an acid solution (page 16) to alter the sharpness when required.

Shannon Marshall, our bar manager, ran with the no-citrus challenge. He adds shrubs made from "kitchen scraps" and infused water kefir to our cocktails; it has been so amazing to watch him create a bar program that Perch is beyond proud of!

Kitchen Program

I remember the time when I was working the pass at a previous restaurant. We couldn't keep up with the orders for the popular sous vide short rib; we were slammed. Near the end of the rush, I noticed a bunch of tiny plastic bags overflowing in a large black plastic garbage bag by the hot side. At that exact moment, I realized how much single-use plastic I had been using in my cooking (which dated back about a decade). Sous vide is an incredibly useful tool in the kitchen toolbox—fantastic for infusions, fermentation, cooking, preserving, etc. I love it. But with so much plastic going into our landfills, I decided I wouldn't use sous vide when I opened my own restaurant. To this day, whether to use sous vide has been one of the biggest internal debates I've had in my head: it would open a world of possibilities and some compostable bags are improving, but I just can't justify it. If biodegradable bags improve significantly, perhaps I'll change my mind. That said, I still use plastic wrap begrudgingly. Our goal is to reduce waste, but it's a gradual process that requires both time and patience. I approach this with baby steps.

My team and I are constantly rethinking waste. Can our kitchen "waste" be turned into a powder, an infusion, a warm consommé to start a meal or a garum? We don't believe organic waste, such as off-cuts and peels, is fit only for compost; we try to repurpose it, whether in the kitchen or for the bar program (page 16).

I believe the only non-Canadian protein I've used is snails from Peconic Escargot out of New York, whose commitment to quality, sustainability and ethical farming practices is second to none (page 54). This is where my thought process may seem confusing. While Canadian products are important to me, ethical farming and fishing practices are even more important. So even if we have access to a Canadian protein, I will choose one from another country if their farmers and fishers are raising or catching the animals more ethically.

Every time we buy something, no matter where it's from, it's recorded, and we're essentially voting. If enough people buy more ethically produced products from outside Canada, it'll prompt the Canadian market to raise its sustainable and ethical standards. However, I won't buy a product if we don't have it in Canada, even if it's ethically farmed or fished. A perfect example of this is langoustine. It's my favourite shellfish, easily, but we don't have them in Canadian waters, so my "vote" of purchasing them, even if ethical, wouldn't have any impact on the Canadian market.

Why It's Important to Us

Our commitment to sustainability and ethical farming is a lot of work, adds an extra level of stress and requires full-time attention. Most of our guests are excited to see us go the extra mile to make Perch as planet friendly as possible. Many love to discuss our approach and ask plenty of questions about our methods and reasoning. As with everything, some people don't see the point and think our commitment is a waste of time. Someone once told me it's a waste of time because it's more performative and doesn't move any real-world sustainability needles. I suppose this is a fair point, but nothing would get started if that were everyone's mindset. Although we may not change the world with our "small" efforts, we don't want to be part of the larger issue. We hope to inspire others to change one or two things in their own world to help preserve our planet—or start a conversation and create a snowball effect. That's an awesome feat and makes all the extra work worthwhile.

Repurposing and Composting

One of the most contentious aspects of fine dining's demand for the perfect knife cut or shape is the amount of food waste it creates. Achieving a perfectly square piece of carrot—which, by nature, is not square—requires countless cuts and scraps. Most often, those pieces end up in the trash. Furthermore, when working in tasting menu–only restaurants, you're usually taught that no ingredient should repeat itself throughout the menu.

We understand the rationale, but the flavour profile of an ingredient can be altered through fermentation or maceration or in vinegars, garums, etc. Why not reuse the "scrap" ingredients by transforming them into something entirely different to place elsewhere on the menu? For a period, we had the same ingredient bookending the menu: our first course and dessert would feature the same ingredients prepared in different ways, using the food scraps from the other dish (for example, a sourdough and squash first course and a sourdough and squash dessert). And if we can't find a home for a food scrap on the tasting menu, we'll look at the cocktail menu. Can we infuse a spirit? Can we turn it into a tea, a bitter or something else to add to a beverage? Some of our best cocktails have had asparagus trim or pea pods in them!

During the colder months, we make a "compost consommé." During prep hours, we add all our food scraps to a pot of simmering water to make a quick stock. Just before service, we strain it, season it and clarify it with agar-agar to create a clear, flavourful broth. This is served at the beginning of the meal while guests look over the drink menu.

That's just one of many repurposing success stories. Our miso-infused brown butter, used to flavour bourbon (Miso Old-Fashioned on the cocktail list), is made into candles with the addition of beeswax. Used fryer oil and spent espresso grounds are combined with vegetable glycerin, potassium hydroxide and citric acid to make our hand soap. We also use spent espresso grounds to make our own coffee liqueur.

The final option for food scraps and waste is compost, and we see this as a way of feeding the soil. Though the most time consuming, Japanese *bokashi* is one of our favourite ways of composting. Food scraps are fermented over time (with some care) and transformed into a nutrient-rich soil amendment. Since the final product is too acidic to dump directly into the garden, it should be combined with soil for a few weeks to break down further. The fermented food also makes an excellent compost tea that can be harvested from the bokashi tub and diluted with water to add straight to your garden!

We also use a self-contained GEME electric composter, which is a container with an auger that can churn up to five kilograms of food waste per day. To set up the machine, you add a packet of microbes that need to be revived and cared for so they can break down the food waste into soil. Still, this product isn't perfect compost (much like bokashi), and it must be added to soil to break down further (when the microbes in the soil interact with those in the compost) and create nutrient-dense soil for your garden.

One issue with these methods is that both final products need to be added to land to complete the process and turn them back into soil. Luckily, many of the farms we work with are happy to take the by-products and add them to future plots to boost the earth's nutrients before the next crop is planted.

While composting isn't a get-out-of-jail-free card when it comes to food waste, it's a very useful tool in our toolkit. The goal is always to repurpose an ingredient or "food waste" before it goes into compost, but compost is a better outcome than the trash. Compost gives back to the earth, creates rich soil and helps grow flavourful, nutrient-dense produce!

The Wild Path: Dining in Nature

Back in 2022, our photographer (and former chef) Sarah Farmer was introduced to Shannon and Pete MacLaggan, the owners of Anupaya Cabin Co. in Laurentian Hills, Ontario. They wanted to host a dinner event along the river, so Sarah reached out to me to join the project and help take on the food menu. During the process of getting the menu written and tested, I became good friends with Shannon and Pete. Both dinners for 2022 and 2023 were done very similarly; however, for the second year Sarah decided to take on a photographer role while Perch created and executed the menu.

Shannon and Pete's transformation of an old hunting camp along the most beautiful section of the Ottawa River into a community of cabins is nothing short of inspiring. Anupaya is on a piece of land with tons of forest and wild foods. One weekend, we built a little fire pit along the river to cook our root vegetables and fish. Shannon's friend Tauney Stinson—a professional beekeeper and owner of Forager Bee—foraged beautiful mushrooms, berries and flowers for our dinner menu, giving the food a real sense of place. Oddly enough, when I was chatting with Tauney after the dinner, we found out that we had met almost seven years prior at our mutual friend's cottage!

The time came for the dinner. For the event, we set a family-style, long table to overlook the river. The twenty-six dinner guests arrived, settled into their cabins and were greeted with a non-alcoholic welcome cocktail. Tauney then guided everyone on a foraging tour of the property, sharing knowledge about the wild foods within the area, what to look for, how to use them and how to engage in ethical foraging. This was followed by a historical discussion of the property by Shannon and Pete as well as an introduction to the resident goats, Kiki and Coco. Once the tours were complete, everyone took a seat at the table for dinner.

The timing worked out perfectly so that dessert was prepared tableside as dusk took hold. After dinner, Sarah led everyone down to the river, where she brewed chai over an open fire and we chatted with guests. It was a great ending to a beautiful day.

The team at Perch looks forward to this dinner series each year, hoping it becomes a long-standing annual tradition. Creating and preparing a dinner in such an idyllic environment, surrounded by interesting people and natural beauty, reminds us of the power of a shared meal and why we love what we do.

WILD PATH DINNER 2022

Bunuelos · Chicken liver · Snail garum

Crudités

Foraged mushroom · Black onion · Reindeer moss

Sunflower seed mac · Pike mousse · Gooseberry

Smoked goose heart · Birch fudge

Garden tomato · *Calendula* · Duck · Goldenrod oil

Catfish · Celeriac · Koji · Milkweed

Cultured butter · Sourdough · Turnip

Salt baked pork · Beets · Foraged mushrooms
White pinecones

Verjus ice-cream sandwiches · Chaga · Sweet fern

Lemon balm cotton candy · Sunflower

Whey caramel taffy · Pineappleweed

Beachside chai

Using These Recipes

I do my best to support local producers and artisans, but recipes are (usually) meant to be broken. If the ingredients aren't accessible to you for whatever reason, feel free to replace them with something local with a similar flavour profile or that you love.

No ingredient is exactly the same twice; the verjus you use might have a completely different pH level than mine. As flavour preferences are subjective and differ from person to person, use these recipes as a foundation. Always taste the product and adjust it to suit your palate or the ingredients being used.

Percentages are my preferred way to calculate ratios within recipes. As you can rarely buy the exact size of ingredient needed, working with ingredient percentages makes it incredibly easy to scale up or down a recipe—and reduce waste. Typically, the hardest-to-find ingredient, or the one least likely to be available in an exact amount, will be the 100% ingredient. As a result, some ingredients may exceed 100% in the recipe.

When calculating the amounts for a recipe, use this formula for ingredients less than 100%:

Ingredient A is 100% at 200 g

Ingredient B is 56%

FORMULA: 200 (ingredient at 100%) × 0.56 (ingredient at 56%) = 112 g (the required amount of Ingredient B)

When figuring out quantities for a recipe, use this formula for ingredients over 100%:

Ingredient A is 100% at 200 g

Ingredient C is 534%

FORMULA: 200 (ingredient at 100%) × 5.34 (ingredient at 534%) = 1068 g (the required amount of Ingredient C)

For ease of reference, I have included both the percentages and the metric weights and rounded the metric figures to the nearest tenth in most instances. For recipes that are better scaled up or down in whole numbers, such as bread loaves or finished cocktails, I have supplied only the metric measurements and omitted percentages.

soil

Rye Bread

MAKES 1 (1-LB) LOAF

There's something incredibly satisfying about starting a meal with fresh bread—especially a dense, flavourful rye bread that's firm enough to carry as much butter as you'd like.

This bread has started every meal at the restaurant since we first opened our doors, and guests will often ask to purchase it. In fact, some staff members at the Danish Embassy buy it from us regularly, stating it's the best they've had outside of their homeland and that it holds its own against true Danish rye bread.

This dough does not require kneading or working: rye is naturally low in gluten, and the loaf is meant to be dense and easy to slice. The rye starter needs to be recently fed twice before making the levain (see Starter Feed).

Seed soak

125 g sunflower seeds
75 g pumpkin seeds

Levain

15 g active rye starter
135 g room-temperature water
90 g fresh-milled rye flour

Rye bread

200 g Levain (see here)
100 g room-temperature water
7 g birch syrup or molasses
Seed Soak (see here), drained and rinsed
200 g fresh-milled rye flour
10 g salt
Non-stick cooking spray, for greasing

Seed soak Combine both ingredients in a lidded container and add enough water to cover them by an inch. Cover and soak for 12 hours.

Levain Combine all ingredients in a lidded container and mix well. Leave to ferment at room temperature for 12 hours.

Rye bread In a bowl, combine levain, water, birch syrup (or molasses) and seed soak. Mix well. Add rye flour and salt. Using a spatula, mix until thick and very sticky.

Grease a 23- × 7.5-cm (9- × 3-inch) loaf pan. Transfer the dough to the prepared pan and smooth the top with a spatula. Cover with a dish towel, then set aside at room temperature for 4–8 hours, until small holes appear on the surface of the dough. The time will depend on the room temperature.

Preheat oven to 200°C (400°F) with a low fan. (If using a convection oven, bake on the lowest fan setting.)

Bake for 45 minutes. Remove the loaf from the tin, then set aside on a wire rack to cool for at least 4 hours. This bread is best when left to cool for at least a day as the flavour will continue to develop after cooling.

Starter Feed

Don't forget to feed your starter! This starter likes a higher hydration than a traditional sourdough starter. (The hydration is 150%.)

Here's an example feeding for this starter:

(50%) 15 g active rye starter
(150%) 45 g room-temperature water
(100%) 30 g fresh-milled rye flour

With this feeding, your starter will peak in 4 hours. From there, you can continue to feed it or refrigerate it for up to a week. Be sure to feed it at least twice, though, before you prepare this rye loaf. To keep the starter alive and active, feed it after preparing the recipe too.

Fresh-Milled Sourdough Loaf

MAKES 1 (1.2-KG) LOAF
FOR A 12-INCH ROUND OR
14-INCH OVAL BANNETON

I had a brief stint working in Montreal for Le Fantôme. Their pastas were served with a generous amount of sauce, and moments after they were brought to the table, the waiters brought over bread to sop up any delicious leftover sauce!

This bread is designed for that exact purpose. It's fluffy, dense and flavourful, yet it doesn't overpower any of the flavour of the sauce.

We bake our sourdough bread in a CHEFTOP MIND.Maps™ combi oven, which is reflected in the instructions below.

120 g active sourdough starter
480 g room-temperature water
450 g stone-milled bread flour
150 g fresh-milled Khorasan flour
12 g salt
White rice flour, for dusting

Combine sourdough starter and water in an Ankarsrum. (Alternatively, use a stand mixer fitted with the appropriate attachment.) Add bread flour and Khorasan flour and mix for 12 minutes on low. Add salt and mix for another 12 minutes. Cover the bowl with a dish towel and set aside to rest for 20 minutes.

Coil fold the dough. Start by wetting your hands with water. Tuck your fingers under the dough and gently lift until you feel tension. Fold the dough over itself, then repeat on the opposite sides. Repeat the 20-minute rest. Fold 3 more times, resting for 20 minutes between each set of coil folds. (So 4 sets in total.)

Bulk ferment the dough for 4–5 hours, until the dough has risen 50%. The dough is ready when it has started to "dome" from the edges of the bowl. The amount of time it takes depends greatly on the room temperature—ideally, 24°C (75°F). Knowing when the dough is ready and risen enough requires practice.

When the dough has risen fully, invert it onto a clean surface. With lightly wet hands, pre-shape the dough into a round. (Avoid using flour during this stage, as it makes final shaping difficult.) Grab the dough gently at the edges to pull and gather into the centre. Using a bench scraper, flip the dough over. Gently tuck the bench scraper under the dough and drag the dough towards you in a half circle until the surface tightens. Repeat the tucking and dragging 2 or 3 more times until the dough holds a round shape. Lightly dust the dough surface with rice flour, then cover with a dish towel and set aside for 20 minutes to rest.

To shape the dough into a boule, repeat the tucking and dragging motion until the surface tension of the dough is tight. (If you'd like to shape the dough into a bâtard, see the instructions in the box.) Flour lightly, then turn into a 12-inch round banneton lined with a cloth, seam side up (the topside of the dough should be facing down into the basket). Cover the seam with the lining cloth or another towel. Refrigerate overnight.

The next day, preheat oven to 260°C (500°F) with the fan on the lowest setting. Place a sheet pan, baking steel or Dutch oven in the oven.

Remove the dough from the fridge and lightly flour the top before gently inverting onto a peel. Using a lame, score your desired pattern. (We do a simple curved slash.)

If you are using a sheet pan or baking steel, use the peel to quickly slide the loaf onto the preheated sheet pan or baking steel in the oven.

If you are using a Dutch oven, remove it from the oven and use the peel to guide the loaf into the Dutch oven. Place the Dutch oven in the oven.

Cover the sheet pan, baking steel or Dutch oven. (We spray the inside of a half hotel pan with water and place it over the loaf once it is in the oven.) Bake for 25 minutes. Uncover the loaf, then reduce oven temperature to 218°C (424°F) and bake for another 20 minutes.

Transfer bread to a cooling rack and set aside for at least 2 hours. Slice.

Bâtard

To shape the dough into a bâtard, lightly flour the top of the pre-shaped dough, then use the bench scraper to flip it over. Gently stretch out the dough into a rectangle, with one of the shorter ends closest to you. Taking the end closest to you, fold it to the midpoint of the rectangle. From this folded section, grab the dough at the left and right, stretch out to the sides, then fold back in to meet at the midpoint. Grab the top of the dough, pull it gently away from you to form a point, then fold to meet the other folded sections.

From here, starting at the end furthest from you, grab the dough edges at the left and right and pull slightly out to the sides. Fold into the centre to meet. Repeat this 4 times along the length of the dough.

Begin to roll the dough into its final shape. Roll the end closest to you a third of the way up, pressing gently along the seam created to form a seal. Repeat this until you reach the end furthest from you, pulling the dough gently towards you once it is completely rolled up to form a tight seal. Try not to push too much on the body of the dough so as not to de-gas the loaf. (For further assistance, look up an online video of how to shape a bâtard loaf.)

Using a bench scraper, transfer the dough to a 12-inch oval banneton, with the seam side facing up. Cover the seam with a lining cloth or a dish towel. Refrigerate overnight.

Fresh-Milled Sourdough Loaf, p.32

Heart City Farm

I've been buying from Heart City Farm since 2016 (though at the time it was called Backyard Edibles), but I met owner Madeleine Maltby long before that when she was still working at Bread by Us in Ottawa. It was my go-to for coffee every morning on my way to work. We chatted often, and she knew I was a cook at one of the local restaurants.

In 2015, she started a unique agricultural business called Backyard Edibles, which created and maintained vegetable gardens in backyards rented from other people. Her partner, Matthew Mason-Phillips, joined the project in 2016. At the time, I was one of their first customers and bought small quantities of whatever was available. They eventually moved into a large warehouse in the heart of Ottawa to create a vertical farm for microgreens and quickly became the favourite microgreen farm for our local restaurant industry. They pushed hard at this model and made the most of it, until they seized an opportunity to acquire acres of farmland with a warehouse in Ottawa's Greenbelt.

Their next chapter became Heart City Farm, growing incredible vegetables, tomatoes and herbs on an expansive piece of land. They also maintained their microgreen operation inside their warehouse. Today, Heart City Farm is one of the most popular local farms working with restaurants and farmers' markets and producing incredible, high-quality produce.

While they may not be certified organic or biodynamic, they practise a lot of these methods and remain committed to similar principles. They don't monocrop, their farm is diversified, and the work is done primarily by hand. They also have a pond to use for water reserve when needed and work closely with the land to make sure that everything they do is net positive for the soil. Their knowledge and drive is truly inspiring and reason enough to support this incredible farm.

Charred Asparagus and Smoked Sturgeon Velouté

This is one of those dishes that came together beautifully. The ingredients for the first course were no longer available, so I had to come up with something quickly. I had excess smoked sturgeon trim in the freezer, first-of-the-season asparagus from Rideau Pines Farm and ramp greens from a local forager. I combined all these ingredients, and the result turned out to be one of the easiest dishes I've ever created. With complexity, freshness and acidity, it's an incredible first course to prepare the palate for the meal.

Smoked sturgeon velouté

- (30%) 30 g butter
- (23%) 23 g leek, white part only, sliced
- (4%) 4 g salt
- (100%) 100 g smoked sturgeon, diced
- (41%) 41 g sake
- (18%) 18 g mirin
- (3.5%) 3.5 g dulse
- (139%) 139 g milk
- (15%) 15 g Lacto-Koji Water (page 176)

Ramp greens emulsion

- (100%) 50 g ramp greens
- (25%) 13 g shallot, roughly chopped
- (150%) 75 g sunflower oil
- (80%) 40 g egg yolks
- (20%) 10 g Dijon mustard
- (15%) 8 g apple cider vinegar
- (4.5%) 2.3 g salt

Tokyo turnips

- 2–3 Tokyo turnips, trimmed with 1-cm (½-inch) stems intact

Asparagus

- 18 asparagus spears

Plating

- Carrot Top Shrub (page 176)
- Toons (microgreen)
- Nasturtium greens
- Tangerine Gem marigold greens
- Nasturtium flower petals

Smoked sturgeon velouté Melt butter in a large pot over medium-low heat. Add leek and salt and sauté for 8 minutes, until translucent. Add sturgeon and cook for 2 minutes. Add sake, mirin and dulse. Simmer for 10 minutes, until reduced by half.

Pour in milk and lacto-koji water. Reduce to very low heat and stir for 10 minutes. Set aside to cool to 40°C (105°F).

Transfer the mixture to a high-powered blender, then blitz on high speed until smooth. Pass through a fine-mesh strainer.

Ramp greens emulsion Place ramp greens, shallot and oil in a high-powered blender. Blend on high speed for 5 minutes. Set aside to cool. Strain.

In a blender, combine egg yolks, mustard, vinegar and salt. Blend on medium speed until emulsified. With the motor running, slowly pour in oil. Transfer to a squeeze bottle.

Tokyo turnips Using a mandoline, thinly slice turnips. Plunge in an ice bath for 10 minutes. Remove from the ice bath, then refrigerate.

Asparagus Trim the woody base of asparagus so that asparagus spears are similar in length.

Bring a saucepan of salted water to a boil. Add asparagus and blanch. Plunge in an ice bath. Place asparagus on a drip tray and set aside to rest at room temperature.

Plating Preheat a Konro grill.

Add to the grill asparagus and lightly grill on all sides.

Place 3 asparagus spears on a tray in the shape of a pyramid. Spray with carrot top shrub. Drizzle ramp greens emulsion over asparagus until coated, leaving asparagus tips exposed.

Using an offset spatula, transfer the charred asparagus to a plate. Rest 3 slices of turnips on the asparagus. Top with 5 toons, 3 nasturtium greens, 3 Tangerine Gem Marigold greens and 3 nasturtium flower petals. Pour velouté next to asparagus. Repeat for the remaining plates.

Sunchoke and Vermouth

Chef Clare Smyth's potato dish at Core inspired a concept that became the foundation for this course. Unsurprisingly, the final dish is nowhere near the original inspiration, which happens frequently with our food. Entirely new originations can start with a single source of inspiration.

Canadian sunchokes are one of my favourite root vegetables. We're lucky to have so many great farms around Ottawa that grow them!

Fried miso-baked sunchokes

(100%) 220 g all-purpose flour, plus extra for dusting
(45%) 99 g salt, enough to coat
(53%) 117 g egg whites
(15%) 33 g navy bean miso
6 sunchokes, cleaned
Sunflower oil, for frying

Crab and sunchoke filling

(50%) 100 g crabmeat, cleaned
(100%) 200 g reserved sunchoke flesh from Fried Miso-Baked Sunchokes (see here)
(1.5%) 3 g tarragon leaves, chiffonade

Clams

(100%) 150 g Lacto-Koji Water (page 176)
(10%) 15 g shallot, sliced
(5%) 8 g garlic, sliced
1 bay leaf
18 live littleneck clams, cleaned

Fried miso-baked sunchokes Preheat oven to 190°C (375°F).

Combine flour and salt and mix in an Ankarsrum. (Alternatively, use a stand mixer fitted with the appropriate attachment.) Add egg whites, miso and just enough water to bring the mixture together to the consistency of pie dough.

Divide the dough into thirds. On a lightly floured work surface, roll out a piece of dough to a thickness of 3 mm (⅛ inch). Place sunchokes on the dough.

Roll out the remaining portions of dough on a sheet of parchment paper. Invert the dough on top of the sunchokes, then peel off the parchment. Press the two sheets of dough together. Transfer to a baking sheet and bake for 40 minutes. (To check doneness, break off a little chunk of the dough where there is a sunchoke and pierce it with a cake tester. It's ready when there is no resistance.) Set aside until cool enough to work with.

Remove sunchokes from the hardened dough (this is easier from the bottom). Take care not to rip sunchokes.

Gently rinse sunchokes, then set aside to dry. Cut off one side of sunchokes, just enough to scoop out the flesh. Reserve the flesh for the filling.

Heat oil in a frying pan over medium-high heat. Add the hollowed sunchokes and gently fry for 5 minutes, until golden and crispy. Take care to retain the shape.

Set aside in a dehydrator set at 40°C (105°F) until needed.

Crab and sunchoke filling Meticulously ensure all shells have been removed from the crabmeat.

Combine all ingredients in a bowl. Using a spatula, mix until smooth but not a paste.

Clams In a saucepan, combine all ingredients except clams and bring to a gentle simmer. Add clams, cover and cook for 5–10 minutes, shaking occasionally, until clams have opened. Remove from heat and set aside until cool enough to handle.

Remove clams from their shells. Discard any clams that have not opened. Reserve the cooking liquid for marinade.

Marinated clams

(33%) 17 g reserved cooking liquid from Clams (see here)
(100%) 50 g verjus
Clams (see here)

Smoked trout roe

(100%) 75 g trout roe

Vermouth sauce

(13%) 13 g butter
(62%) 62 g leek, white and pale green parts only, sliced
(4%) 4 g garlic, sliced
(3%) 3 g salt
(100%) 100 g Dolin Blanc Vermouth de Chambéry (not dry!)
1 bay leaf
(130%) 130 g milk
(27%) 27 g clotted cream
(37%) 37 g sour cream

Marinated clams Strain the reserved cooking liquid into a saucepan and simmer until reduced by half. Set aside to cool.

Combine cooking liquid and verjus in a bowl. Add clams, then set aside until needed.

Smoked trout roe Place trout roe in a container with a lid, pop one corner of the lid up and place the nozzle of a smoking gun in the container. Add smoke. Once the container is filled with smoke, turn off the smoking gun, remove the nozzle and close the lid tightly. Let sit for 5 minutes, then repeat once.

Vermouth sauce Melt butter in a saucepan over medium heat. Add leek, garlic and salt and cook for 8–12 minutes, until softened. Add vermouth and bay leaf, bring to a simmer and cook for 5 minutes. Stir in milk, clotted cream and sour cream and simmer for another 5 minutes.

Remove bay leaf, transfer the mixture to a high-powered blender and blitz until smooth. Strain through a fine-mesh strainer.

Plating Remove the hollowed sunchokes from the dehydrator. Place 3 marinated clams inside each sunchoke, one at each end and one in the middle. Fill with crab and sunchoke filling, packing it in.

Invert a sunchoke, open side down, in each bowl. Place smoked trout roe around the sunchoke.

In a saucepan, bring vermouth sauce to a simmer. Pour around sunchoke.

 Sunchoke and Vermouth, p.40

Mushroom and Rye, p.44

Mushroom and Rye

Chef Jason Gloor once made a vinegar soup dish when we were working together. People either loved or hated the high acidity, and I was part of the camp who loved it. I wanted to create a dish with lots of depth, smoke and high acidity using Jason's dish as inspiration.

This was our most divisive dish, garnering a wide range of reactions from guests. The broth in this recipe has a ton of background notes to keep it savoury and warming and a sharp acidity to engage the palate. Again, diners either loved it or hated it.

Whenever I thought about changing the dish, a journalist would want to write about it—so I kept extending it until the publication of the articles. And for that reason, this dish had a much longer lifespan than I'd expected. It was also a great way to use up excess wine as we would make our own vinegar for this course.

Haskap vinegar	(100%)	454 g haskap, juiced
		Chardonnay yeast (according to package instructions)
		Vinegar SCOBY
Dulse-infused rice wine vinegar	(100%)	454 g rice wine vinegar
	(8.8%)	40 g dulse
Smoked butter	(100%)	50 g butter, room temperature
Rye berries	(100%)	175 g toasted rye
	(200%)	350 g water
Charred cabbage purée	(100%)	200 g green cabbage, coarsely chopped
	(49%)	98 g brown butter
	(2%)	4 g salt
Rye berries and cabbage	(100%)	300 g Rye Berries (see here)
	(43%)	129 g Charred Cabbage Purée (see here)

Haskap vinegar Combine haskap and chardonnay yeast (use the proper amount according to package instructions) and ferment for 14 days.

Add vinegar SCOBY, cover with a cloth and set aside at room temperature for 1 month, until the pH is less than 3.

Dulse-infused rice wine vinegar Bring vinegar to a simmer in a saucepan.

Place dulse in a heatproof container. Pour in the hot vinegar. Set aside at room temperature for at least 7 days to infuse.

Smoked butter Spread a thin layer of butter in a container. Pop one corner of the lid up and place the nozzle of a smoking gun in the container. Add smoke. Once the container is filled with smoke, turn off the smoking gun, remove the nozzle and close the lid tightly. Let sit for 5 minutes, then repeat once.

Rye berries Combine both ingredients in a pressure cooker. Cook on high for 30 minutes. Force release. Strain, then transfer to a tray to cool.

Charred cabbage purée Preheat a grill.

Preheat oven to 190°C (375°F).

Add cabbage to the grill and char all over until dark. Place in the oven and brown until some areas are charred.

Place in a high-powered blender, then add brown butter and salt and blitz. Pass through a fine-mesh strainer.

Rye berries and cabbage Combine both ingredients in a saucepan and warm through.

Camelina-roasted mushrooms	(100%)	240 g oyster mushroom
	(15%)	36 g camelina oil
		Salt, to season
Roasted garlic dashi	(100%)	250 g Seaweed Water (page 175)
	(22%)	55 g Dulse-Infused Rice Wine Vinegar (see here)
	(18%)	45 g mirin
	(12%)	30 g shoyu
	(1%)	2.5 g salt
	(6%)	15 g roasted garlic
Pickled sea lettuce	(33%)	33 g sea lettuce
	(100%)	100 g rice vinegar
	(40%)	40 g mirin
	(40%)	40 g sake
	(22%)	22 g water
	(40%)	40 g sugar
Toasted heartnuts	(100%)	50 g heartnuts
Plating		Julienned leek, about 2.5 cm (1 inch) in length, for garnish
		Micro radishes, for garnish
		Marigold flower petals, for garnish

Camelina-roasted mushrooms Preheat oven to 175°C (347°F).

Combine all ingredients in a bowl. Transfer to a baking sheet and roast for 10 minutes, until lightly browned. Set aside to cool.

Roasted garlic dashi Combine all ingredients except garlic in a saucepan. Bring to a simmer. Add garlic and set aside for 5 minutes.

Transfer to a high-powered blender and blitz on high speed until smooth. Strain through an oil filter. Refrigerate until cooled.

Pickled sea lettuce Soak sea lettuce in water for 10 minutes. Drain.

Meanwhile, combine the remaining ingredients in a saucepan and bring to a boil. Pour the liquid over sea lettuce, then set aside to cool.

Toasted heartnuts Preheat oven to 175°C (347°F).

Break heartnuts, reserving the nuts. Place nuts on a baking sheet and roast for 7–12 minutes, until golden and fragrant.

Plating Place rye berries and cabbage on each bowl.

Melt smoked butter in a frying pan over medium-high heat. Add camelina-roasted mushrooms and sauté until heated through. Deglaze with 30 mL of haskap vinegar. Place over rye berries and cabbage.

Garnish each bowl with 3 pickled sea lettuce, leek, 7 micro radishes and 3 marigold flower petals. Using a rotary cheese grater, grate a few heartnuts over mushrooms.

Pour hot (not simmering) roasted garlic dashi broth into the bowl so it comes halfway up the rye berries.

Broccoli and Sea Buckthorn

This understated dish is one of my favourite creations and a reminder not to take a dish too far with ingredients. I wanted the broccoli stem to take centre stage in a dish, but I thought I'd need a lot of small background notes to make the dish eat well.

I added a few components and tasted it to determine where I needed it to go. Two bites in, I knew I had to stop it right there—it's very simple in appearance but wildly complex in flavour! This is a great example of our ethos, taking something that most would regard as waste and making it the star of the dish.

Broccoli stems

2 broccolis

Broccoli purée

(100%)	150 g broccoli florets and trimmings (not peelings)
(10%)	15 g whipping cream
(5%)	8 g butter
(8%)	12 g Shio Koji (page 176)
(1.75%)	2.6 g salt

Umami powder

(100%)	75 g dehydrated broccoli trimmings
(66%)	50 g dehydrated beurre blanc reduction solids from Pike Agnolotti Pasta (page 114)
(31%)	23 g nori
(17%)	13 g sea salt

Sweetened sea buckthorn juice

(100%)	100 g sea buckthorn juice (juiced through a macerating juicer)
(47%)	47 g sugar

Sea buckthorn and camelina emulsion

(100%)	100 g Sweetened Sea Buckthorn Juice (see here)
(100%)	100 g camelina oil

Plating

(100%)	200 g Seaweed Water (page 175)
(25%)	50 g butter

Broccoli stems Remove florets, keeping the stem intact as much as possible. Reserve florets and trimmings for broccoli purée. Quarter the stems and cut each stem so it lays flat.

Bring a saucepan of salted water to a boil. Add stems and blanch for 4–6 minutes, until cooked. Shock in an ice bath. Transfer stems to a container.

Broccoli purée Bring a saucepan of salted water to a boil. Add broccoli florets and trimmings and blanch for 4 minutes, until soft. Drain.

In a separate saucepan, combine cream and butter and heat on low heat until butter has melted.

In a high-powered blender, combine broccoli florets and trimmings, cream-butter mixture and shio koji. Blitz until smooth. Season with salt. Pass through a fine-mesh strainer. Transfer to a squeeze bottle. Refrigerate to cool.

Umami powder Combine all ingredients in a high-powered blender and blitz to a powder.

Sweetened sea buckthorn juice Combine both ingredients in a saucepan and bring to a simmer. Strain through a fine-mesh strainer.

Sea buckthorn and camelina emulsion Combine both ingredients in a high-powered blender and blend to emulsify.

Plating Bring seaweed water to a simmer in a saucepan. Add butter and whisk until melted. Add broccoli stems and cook until warmed through. Place stems on a tray, then dust with umami powder until entirely covered.

Place stems on each plate. Add dots of broccoli purée next to them. Pour sea buckthorn and camelina emulsion between the dots of purée.

Beets and Fennel

When we first opened, we wanted to have a small lounge/bar area for drinks and small plates. That way, walk-ins could show up and have a glass of wine or a cocktail, maybe a plate of food and some good laughs and conversations with us. The open-plan room was split in two—more in theory than in practice—with sixteen seats on one side for the tasting menu and twelve seats in the lounge area. Very quickly, the tasting menu began selling out and we weren't getting the anticipated foot traffic for the lounge, so we eventually expanded the dining area and dropped the lounge to accommodate more tasting menu patrons.

This was the only lounge dish we brought over to the tasting menu side. These chewy beets give you an entirely unique experience with the beet flavour and texture. So while they're time consuming to make, the result is worth the effort.

Chewy beets

3 beets

Caramelized salsify

3 salsifies, skin on and washed
(100%) 50 g butter

Fennel cream

Sunflower oil, for frying
(43%) 97 g fennel, sliced (divided)
(18%) 40.5 g yellow onion
(3.6%) 8 g garlic, sliced
(2%) 4.5 g ginger, sliced
(10%) 23 g white wine
(100%) 225 g buttermilk
Salt, to taste
(0.7%) 1.6 g Ultratex 3

Fennel oil

(100%) 10 g fennel fronds
(1103%) 110 g sunflower oil

Absinthe stock

(100%) 100 g Dillon's Absinthe
(133%) 133 g water
(63%) 63 g honey

Plating

Butter, for frying
Fennel pollen (dehydrated fennel flowers), for dusting
Small anise hyssop leaves, for garnish
Flowers: pea, bean and snapdragon, for garnish

Chewy beets Preheat oven to 177°C (350°F).

Roast beets for 3 hours, until tender. Peel and quarter. Place them in a dehydrator set at 70°C (158°F) for 4 hours.

Caramelized salsify Preheat a frying pan over medium heat. Add salsifies and sear, rotating frequently, until they can be pierced with a cake tester with little resistance.

Turn off the heat. Add butter and agitate the pan to roll salsifies in the foaming butter. Set aside to fully cool.

Gently remove any burnt skin from salsifies. Transfer to a cutting board and halve lengthwise. Cut into 2.5-cm (1-inch) segments.

Fennel cream Heat oil in a frying pan over medium heat. Add 61 g of fennel, onion, garlic and ginger and sauté until translucent. Add wine and reduce by half.

Pour in buttermilk and bring to a simmer. Stir in 36 g of fennel and gently simmer for 8 minutes, until softened.

Transfer to a high-powered blender and blitz until smooth. With the motor running on medium speed, add salt and Ultratex. Pass through a fine-mesh strainer.

Fennel oil Combine both ingredients in a high-powered blender and blitz on high speed for 8 minutes. Strain through an oil filter.

Absinthe stock Combine all ingredients in a saucepan and bring to a simmer. Keep warm.

Plating In a saucepan, reheat salsifies in a little butter, then transfer to individual plates.

Add beets to the saucepan of absinthe stock and warm through. Place beets between salsifies, then dust with fennel pollen.

Bring fennel cream to a light simmer. Calculate 25% of the amount of fennel cream, then measure this amount in fennel oil and add to cream. Pour the mixture onto the plates. Garnish with anise hyssop and flowers.

Bower Farm

Small but beautiful, Bower Farm has become one of our most beloved farms. David and Amanda Bower grow some of the most prestigious produce, and we buy from them as much as possible.

For one, their pineapple ground cherries, also known as physalis, have become a staple in our "signature bite" Scallop Macaron (page 124). The ginger at the farm is head and shoulders above any other ginger I've ever tasted. Plus, their towering fig trees yield the juiciest and most flavourful figs.

They also have an extremely well-cared-for flock of chickens. Unfortunately, as the eggs are ungraded and the flock isn't large enough to be commercially certified by the government, we can't use them at the restaurant (see page 74 for more on our eggs). However, I personally buy them for consumption at home because they are some of the tastiest eggs I've ever had.

They also have several bee hives set up behind the property, creating an environment to support their farm from pollination to fruit production. These hives are cared for by the Barking Bee Company, which also produces the honey we use most in the restaurant.

Working with David is such a great experience—his passion for plants, the soil and the earth that he cares for is contagious. I can always rely on the produce to be in perfect condition from healthy soil. Crops are regularly rotated to ensure that specific nutrients aren't completely depleted from the earth and are given the time to replenish.

David and Amanda grow produce based on the needs of their land, which results in wonderful fruit and vegetables that have been featured on the Perch menu since we first opened.

Squash and Sourdough

I once bought a ton of beautiful snails from Peconic Escargot in New York and made an incredible garum with so much depth of flavour. I then turned it into a sweet glaze, using aromatics and golden caramel. When we tasted the end "garamel," my brain went to pairing it with a nice piece of squash. We also had sourdough bread scraps from service, so I began playing around with them to make a porridge-like sauce.

This dish became the perfect starting course for our autumn menu, when temperatures began to drop. It is one of my favourite creations.

Snail garamel

(225%)	100 g sugar
(42%)	19 g water (A)
(12%)	5.3 g verjus
(63%)	28 g shallot, sliced
(9%)	4 g garlic, sliced
(2.5%)	1.1 g aji charapita pepper, sliced
(0.75%)	0.3 g ground sumac
(0.25%)	0.1 g toasted alder catkin, broken up
(100%)	44.5 g snail Garum (page 178)
(42%)	19 g water (B)

Confit butternut squash

Lard
1 butternut squash, cut into large batons
Snail Garamel (see here)

Puffed wild rice

Sunflower oil, for deep-frying
(100%) 50 g wild rice
Salt, to season

Puffed amaranth

(100%) 50 g amaranth seeds

Sourdough porridge

(20%)	15 g butter
(50%)	38 g shallot, sliced
(10%)	8 g garlic, sliced
(2%)	1.5 g salt
(21%)	16 g Corn Cob–Infused Whisky (page 162)
(13%)	10 g miso
(71%)	53 g poultry stock
(140%)	105 g oat milk
(100%)	75 g sourdough scraps, dried out

Snail garamel In a saucepan, combine sugar, water (A) and verjus and cook over medium heat for 8–12 minutes, until dark amber in colour. Do not burn. Remove from heat.

Add shallot, garlic, pepper, sumac and alder and gently stir to fully incorporate. Add water (B) to snail garum, then gently add the mixture to garamel and gently stir. Cook over medium heat until bubbles form. Remove from heat, then set aside for 20 minutes. Strain and refrigerate until needed.

Confit butternut squash Melt lard in a large frying pan over medium heat, until it reaches 120°C (248°F). Add squash and roast for 20–30 minutes, until cooked through with some bite. Set aside until cooled.

Store in snail garamel until needed.

Puffed wild rice Heat oil in a saucepan to 205°C (401°F). Working in batches, add wild rice and deep-fry until puffed. (This happens very quickly!) Transfer to a paper towel–lined plate. Season with salt. Repeat with the remaining batches.

Puffed amaranth Heat a saucepan over high heat. Add amaranth seeds and gently shake the pan to prevent seeds from burning. Heat until puffed. Transfer to a tray.

Sourdough porridge Melt butter in a saucepan over medium heat. Add shallot, garlic and salt. Sauté for 5 minutes, until translucent. Add whisky and miso and cook until almost completely evaporated. Pour in stock and oat milk and bring to a simmer. Add sourdough and cook for 5 minutes, until bread is fully softened.

Working in small batches, transfer the mixture to a high-powered blender and blitz. Pass through a fine-mesh drum sieve.

Apple slices

1 Granny Smith apple, sliced
Acidulated water, to cover

Plating

Butter, for frying
Salt, to season
Lots of Tangerine Gem marigold petals

Apple slices Combine both ingredients in a bowl and set aside for 5 minutes. Remove apples from the solution and hold in the bowl until needed.

Plating Place a dollop of sourdough porridge on one side of each plate. Using a spoon, create a small divot in the centre. Using a blowtorch, toast the porridge until lightly charred.

Place apple slices, no wider or longer than the squash, on the plate next to the porridge. Pour in enough snail garamel to fill the divot.

Melt butter in a frying pan over medium heat. Add squash and heat until warmed through. Place squash on a resting tray. Brush top of squash with more snail garamel and season with salt.

Cover squash with puffed amaranth, puffed wild rice and marigold petals. Carefully place squash on top of apples.

 Squash and Sourdough, p.54

Ramp Spaghettini, p.58

Ramp Spaghettini

Supporting the true artisans that grow or catch our food is important to us, and it is our goal to prioritize small farms and fisheries. Foggy Shoals Fish Co. out of Bonavista, Newfoundland, fits our criteria perfectly. During a conversation one day with owner Paul Babineau, he mentioned that divers would be able to hand harvest the sea urchin in the upcoming week. The conceptualization of a dish started that day.

The flavour of whole live sea urchin is a thing of beauty. Unfortunately, an issue with sea urchins is how long they stay pristine after they're out of the water. (Pre-shucked sea urchins tend to be chemically preserved to prolong the shelf life.)

When making a sauce, you lose the sea urchin's delicate, mousse-like texture, but its flavour remains intact, allowing you to enjoy sea urchin over a longer period. This sauce recipe was tested several times, but once we nailed it, we immediately turned it into a pasta sauce with a ramp greens pasta and fresh-milled sourdough on the side to sop up all the extra sauce on the plate—made for that exact purpose.

Koji-fermented kohlrabi juice

(100%) 250 g kohlrabi juice
(50%) 125 g Koji (page 175)
(3%) 8 g sea salt

Cured duck breast

(100%) 250 g salt
(100%) 250 g sugar
(5%) 13 g ground sumac
(3%) 8 g sea buckthorn greens
(2%) 5 g alder catkin, toasted
(2%) 5 g bay leaf
1 duck breast

Pasta dough

(121%) 85 g egg yolks
(100%) 70 g ramp greens, chiffonade
(86%) 60 g blanched ramp greens
(410%) 287 g all-purpose flour, plus extra for dusting
(1%) 0.7 g salt
Semolina, to coat

Koji-fermented kohlrabi juice Combine all ingredients in a high-powered blender and blend until smooth.

Pour the mixture into a fermentation jar that's fitted with an airlock, then press plastic wrap onto the surface of the liquid. Seal the jar. Set aside at room temperature for 5 days.

Strain through cheesecloth into a container.

Leftover juice can be stored in the fridge for 5 days or the freezer for 3 months. (The pulp can be used to make a Kohlrabi Shrub [page 177].)

Cured duck breast Combine all ingredients except duck in a Thermomix and blitz until fine.

Clean any excess sinew off duck. Cover it with the salt cure, then refrigerate for 5 days.

Rinse off the cure, then pat duck dry and place on a rack. Place in a dehydrator set at 60°C (140°F) overnight. Refrigerate until needed.

Pasta dough In a high-powered blender, combine egg yolks and both ramps and blitz until smooth.

Combine flour and salt in an Ankarsrum. (Alternatively, use a stand mixer fitted with the appropriate attachment.) With the motor still running, pour in the wet ingredients. If needed, add more flour until the dough has the right consistency.

Transfer the dough to a clean work surface lightly dusted with flour, then finish kneading the dough by hand. Wrap, then rest for at least 1 hour.

Starting at the widest setting of a pasta roller, roll through the pasta dough until you reach setting #4 (roughly midway). Cut the dough into 25-cm (10-inch) long sheets. Roll through the spaghettini attachment. Transfer to a tray with semolina to coat. Divide into 45-g portions.

Confit eggplant

Salt, to season
1 eggplant, peeled and sliced into thin rounds
Sunflower oil, for frying
(100%) 225 g white wine vinegar
(22%) 50 g verjus
(60%) 135 g camelina oil
(60%) 135 g sunflower oil

Stock base

(10%) 14 g butter
(21%) 29 g shallot, sliced
(2%) 2.8 g garlic, sliced
(16%) 22 g white wine (preferably Sémillon)
(0.62%) ~1 g aji charapita pepper, sliced
(100%) 140 g poultry stock
(18%) 25 g verjus
(22%) 31 g Lacto-Koji Water (page 176)

Sea urchin base

(100%) 150 g sea urchin
(56%) 84 g high-fat sour cream

Sea urchin sauce

(100%) 200 g Stock Base (see here)
(100%) 200 g Sea Urchin Base (see here)
(43%) 86 g butter
(39%) 78 g whipping cream
(50%) 100 g verjus
(28%) 56 g Koji-Fermented Kohlrabi Juice (see here)

Plating

Smoked sea salt, to season
Fennel fronds, for garnish

Confit eggplant Peel eggplant and slice into 5–6-mm (¼-inch) thick rounds. Salt both sides of eggplant slices and set aside for 1 hour on a perforated pan to release water.

Wipe excess salt and water off eggplant and dice to a medium size.

Heat sunflower oil in a frying pan over medium heat. Add eggplant and cook for 3 minutes. Add vinegar and verjus and stir for 1 minute. Add camelina oil and the remaining sunflower oil. Remove from heat.

Stock base Melt butter in a saucepan over medium heat. Add shallot and garlic and sweat for 6–8 minutes, until translucent. Add wine and pepper and simmer until reduced by half. Add stock and simmer for another 10 minutes.

Pour in verjus and lacto-koji water. Transfer to a high-powered blender and blend on high speed until smooth. Pass through a fine-mesh strainer.

Sea urchin base Combine both ingredients in a high-powered blender and blend. Refrigerate until needed. The base will last only a few hours in this form.

Sea urchin sauce Bring stock base to a simmer in a saucepan. Whisk in sea urchin base, then butter until it has melted. Whisk in cream. Stir in verjus and koji-fermented kohlrabi juice.

Plating Bring a large saucepan of salted water to a boil. Lower pasta into the boiling water and cook for 3 minutes.

Warm up sea urchin sauce in a separate pan.

Drain pasta, then place in the heated sea urchin sauce. Toss to coat. Place pasta on each plate, then add extra sauce on top.

Using a slotted spoon, remove eggplant from the frying pan. Place as much eggplant as you'd like over pasta. Season with smoked sea salt. Using a sharp rasp grater, grate cured duck over pasta. Garnish with fennel fronds.

Squab Liver Mousse Bunuelos

Making our sourdough bread yields an excess of discard that would either go into the compost or be brought home to make pancakes for breakfast. We needed a solution that would reincorporate the discard on the menu, so we tried making a shell out of the discard in a bunuelo stamp. After a few attempts, we finally got it to work (and not just disintegrate in the fryer). It has a beautiful and crispy, yet delicate, texture and a mild sweetness with a little sour tang.

Fermented peach powder

Reserved peach solids from Lacto-Peach Juice in Lost in Migration (page 166)

Peach and chamomile fluid gel

- (100%) 750 g peaches
- (32%) 240 g charred peaches
- Sunflower oil, for frying
- (7%) 53 g Torpedo onion, sliced
- (0.5%) 4 g salt
- (5%) 38 g mead
- (2%) 15 g Yellow Chartreuse
- (2%) 15 g honey
- Agar-agar (total weight to be determined below)

Squab liver mousse

- (100%) 200 g squab liver, soaked overnight
- Sunflower oil, for frying
- (7%) 14 g shallot, sliced
- (5%) 10 g garlic, sliced
- Salt, to season
- (3%) 6 g whisky
- (25%) 50 g cubed butter, cold
- (25%) 50 g whipping cream, cold

Fermented peach powder Place peach solids in a dehydrator set at 45°C (113°F) for 36 hours or until completely dried.

Blitz in a dry high-powered blender until a fine powder is achieved.

Peach and chamomile fluid gel Juice both peaches, reserving the combined pulp.

Heat a small amount of oil in a saucepan over medium-high heat. Add onion and salt and sauté for 7 minutes, until translucent. Pour in mead, Chartreuse and honey and bring to a simmer. Add peach juice and pulp and cook for another 5 minutes, stirring continuously. Remove from heat. Strain through cheesecloth and set aside to cool.

Weigh the liquid, then return it to a saucepan. Whisk in 1% of agar-agar and bring to a simmer. Transfer to a container, then set aside to cool. Refrigerate until completely set.

Place the mixture in a high-powered blender and blitz until smooth. Pass through a fine-mesh strainer. Transfer to a squeeze bottle.

Squab liver mousse Note: For the mousse to blend properly, we make more than needed.

Carefully devein squab liver and set aside.

Heat oil in a frying pan over medium heat. Add shallot and garlic and sauté for 8 minutes, until translucent. Season with salt. Add squab liver and gently cook for a few minutes but do not allow it to colour. Pour in whisky and flambé.

Once whisky is burned off, stir in butter and cream. Bring to a very gentle simmer. Remove from heat and cool to 45°C (113°F).

Pour the mixture into a high-powered blender and blend until smooth. Pass through a fine-mesh strainer into a container. Refrigerate until cold.

Transfer mousse to a piping bag; no piping tip is needed.

Bunuelos

(30%) 30 g sourdough discard
(100%) 100 g water
(50%) 50 g all-purpose flour
Neutral oil, for frying

Plating

Cornflower petals
Mini Gem marigold petals

Bunuelos Note: Because this subrecipe depends so heavily on your discard, there is no perfect recipe—a bit of trial and error is required. However, you can use the ingredient ratios as a starting point, which we also generally use at the restaurant.

Combine all ingredients except oil in a bowl and adjust quantities as necessary until the consistency is thick but loose.

Place a bunuelo stamp in a countertop fryer, add oil and set to high heat. Once oil and stamp are hot, carefully remove the stamp from oil and dip into the batter. Place the stamp in the fryer for a few seconds—the discard shell should pop off easily on its own or with tweezers. Fry the batter until the bubbles subside. Transfer to a paper towel–lined drip tray. Repeat to make 6 bunuelos total. If possible, place in a dehydrator set at 45°C (113°F) until needed.

Plating Cut the tip off the piping bag so that a small amount of mousse comes out at a time. Pipe mousse into each bunuelo, then dust the entire bunuelo with fermented peach powder. Place a dot of fluid gel at each of the meeting points on bunuelo. Place one cornflower petal on each fluid gel dot and a Mini Gem marigold flower in the centre of bunuelo.

Squab Liver Mousse Bunuelos, p.60

UNOX

land

2

Quail Chawanmushi

We knew we wanted to offer coffee at Perch. Luckily, our friend Kevin Joanisse started his own roastery, Lulo, in Ottawa and roasts some of the best coffee in Canada. I had an urge to use the coffee "waste" from the farm that produced the coffee we were using, Wilfredo who owns and operates Finca Alcatraz in Oporapa, Huila, Colombia.

We made a beautiful tea from cascara, the dried skin of coffee cherries, to add depth and nuance to the chawanmushi.

Aged quail breast

6 quail breasts
Koji, dried (page 175), for dusting

Mushroom confit

(100%) 200 g sunflower oil, plus 2 Tbsp for frying
(50%) 100 g shallot, brunoise
(15%) 30 g tomato paste
(18%) 36 g black garlic paste
(12%) 24 g miso
(5%) 10 g gochujang
(2%) 4 g dried mushroom powder
(100%) 200 g mushroom, brunoise
(30%) 60 g Seaweed Water (page 175)

Cascara-infused dashi "syrup"

(100%) 125 g soy sauce
(83%) 104 g mirin
(50%) 63 g sea buckthorn juice
(33%) 41 g sherry vinegar
(33%) 41 g honey
(10%) 13 g coffee cherries

Koji dashi

(100%) 175 g Seaweed Water (page 175)
(10%) 18 g mirin
(5%) 9 g soy sauce
(15% of above total weight) ~30 g Koji, dried (page 175)

Koji dashi custard

(100%) 175 g Koji Dashi (see here)
(75%) 131 g eggs

Plating

Sunflower oil, for frying
Butter, for basting
Flake sea salt, to season
1 scallion, thinly sliced on the bias, for garnish

Aged quail breast Remove breasts from the carcass. (The carcass can be used for a stock or consommé.) Dust with dried koji and refrigerate for 3–6 days.

Mushroom confit Heat 2 tablespoons of oil in a frying pan over medium-high heat. Add shallot and sweat for 12 minutes, until translucent. Add tomato paste and cook for 5 minutes. Stir in black garlic paste, miso and gochujang and cook for another 5 minutes.

Add dried mushroom powder. Add mushroom and sauté for 10 minutes. Pour in seaweed water and cook until nearly dry *(au sec)*. Pour in 200 g of oil, reduce heat to low and cook for 45 minutes.

Cascara-infused dashi "syrup" In a saucepan, combine all ingredients except coffee cherries. Bring to a boil. Remove from heat, then stir in coffee cherries. Set aside to cool.

Koji dashi Combine all ingredients except dried koji in a saucepan and bring to a boil. Remove from heat, then add dried koji and steep for 10 minutes. Strain.

Koji dashi custard Preheat a combi oven to 99°C (210°F).

Combine eggs and koji dashi in a bowl and mix well to make the custard base. Strain through a fine-mesh strainer. Pour 50 g of the base each into 6 heatproof bowls.

Steam in the combi oven on the top rack for 5 minutes and 30 seconds with full steam.

Plating Heat oil in a frying pan over medium heat. Add quail, skin side down, and brown for 5 minutes, until skin is seared. Flip quail and pan-fry for 4 minutes. Baste with butter. Transfer quail to a tray and set aside to rest for 4 minutes.

Slice quail in bite-size slices, then season with sea salt.

To serve, pour dashi syrup over the custard. Add mushroom confit to the centre. Top with sliced quail breast. Garnish with a few scallion slices.

Rabbit and Balsam Fir Sauce

We're quite lucky to be so close to Quebec, which has so many incredible farms. Many of them promote ethical farming, giving their animals more space to roam and better overall care. Mariposa Farm (who are in Ontario but work with a lot of Quebec farms) offer products from their own farm as well as others that meet their standards and believe in "hardcore sustainability," so you know you're getting great products. When they sent me a message saying they would be offering fresh rabbit from Quebec, I made sure it was on the menu.

Rabbit

1 rabbit
Shio Koji (page 176), to coat

Shallot mix

Sunflower oil, for frying
(100%) 100 g shallot, brunoise
(13%) 13 g garlic, microplaned
(75%) 75 g sweet vermouth

Roulade

(100%) 400 g reserved ground rabbit from Rabbit (see here)
(25%) 100 g Shallot Mix (see here)
(8%) 32 g celery, brunoise
(0.75%) 3 g Activa® RM, plus extra for dusting
Reserved rabbit saddle from Rabbit (see here)
Neutral oil, for brushing
Salt, to season

Rabbit Start by butchering the rabbit. Debone the rabbit, then grind the leg meat. Reserve both this and the saddle for the roulade.

Separate the loins from each other. Gently slice the belly skin in a crosshatch pattern, taking care not to cut through the skin. Coat in shio koji, then refrigerate for 4 hours. Rinse, then pat dry with paper towels.

Preheat oven to 215°C (419°F).

Place the bones on a baking sheet and roast till nicely browned.

Transfer the bones to a stockpot and cover with a couple inches of water. Simmer for 4–6 hours, skimming periodically. Strain through an oil filter placed in a cone-shaped strainer and let the liquid cool overnight in the fridge.

The next day, remove any fat cap from the stock. In a stockpot over medium heat, reduce the liquid to 25% of the original amount. Strain through a fine-mesh strainer. Reserve.

Shallot mix Heat oil in a frying pan over medium heat. Add shallot and garlic and sauté for 7 minutes, until shallot is transparent. Add vermouth and cook for 4 minutes, until reduced and syrupy.

Roulade In a bowl, combine ground rabbit, shallot mix, celery and Activa® RM. Gently dust the flesh side of the saddle, including the belly skin, with Activa® RM. Place the ground rabbit mixture over the belly of the saddle. Roll saddle up tightly using plastic wrap. Wrap tightly in the plastic wrap, then tie both ends. Refrigerate overnight.

Preheat a combi oven to 99°C (210°F).

Remove roulade from the plastic wrap. Brush oil over one side of a sheet of aluminum foil. Sprinkle it with salt. Place roulade at one end of the sheet and roll tightly.

Add the wrapped roulade to a frying pan over medium-high high and roll it every 2–3 minutes until seared on all sides. (Do not unwrap it.)

Insert a probe through the thickest part of the roulade. Cook in the combi oven at full steam for about 29 minutes with the probe set to 58°C (136°F). Once the temperature is reached, leave in the oven for another 2 minutes. Remove, then place on a rack and cool quickly in the fridge.

Once cooled, unwrap foil and slice roulade into 1-cm (½-inch) thick medallions.

Celiac and leek pavé

(100%) 200 g whipping cream
(10%) 20 g birch syrup
(5%) 10 g miso
(1%) 2 g salt, plus extra to season
3 medium-large celeriac, thinly sliced on meat slicer
Butter, for dotting
1 leek, green part only, cut lengthwise and blanched

Caramelized parsnip purée

(100%) 500 g parsnip
(15%) 75 g melted butter
(15%) 75 g water
(1.5%) 8 g salt
(0.5%) 2.5 g baking soda

Balsam fir sauce

Sunflower oil, for frying
(14%) 56 g red onion, sliced
(1.5%) 6 g garlic, sliced
Salt, to season
(35%) 140 g reserved solids from Quince-Infused Whisky (page 158)
(1.5%) 6 g sugar
(8%) 32 g red wine
(100%) 400 g reserved rabbit stock from Rabbit (see here)
(42%) 168 g salal berry juice
(19%) 76 g verjus, plus extra to season
(1.5%) 6 g dried balsam fir buds
(1%) 4 g Ultratex 3

Celeriac and leek pavé Preheat oven to 205°C (401°F). Line a one-third hotel pan with a sheet of parchment paper with a 10-cm (4-inch) overhang.

In a bowl, combine cream, birch syrup, miso and salt. Add celeriac and mix to coat. Arrange a single layer of the celeriac mixture in the prepared pan. Add a few knobs of butter. Repeat to create several layers. Season with salt.

Add a layer of leek. Repeat with more layers of celeriac and butter. Fold over the excess parchment paper to cover the top, then cover with aluminum foil. Bake for 1 hour. Set aside to cool.

Place a heavy weight on top of the pavé, then refrigerate overnight. Cut into 2- × 5-cm (¾- × 2-inch) portions.

Caramelized parsnip purée Note: To create enough pressure in the pressure cooker, this subrecipe makes more than required.

Peel parsnip and reserve for crispy parsnip skins. Chop parsnip and place in a pressure cooker. Add the remaining ingredients. This recipe can be a little tricky: You want to make sure the butter does not solidify at all before the pressure cooker turns on. If you're having issues with this, add 50 g of water to the pressure cooker.

Cook on high for 50 minutes. Force release.

Transfer the mixture to a high-powered blender and blitz until smooth. Pass through a fine-mesh strainer. Let cool. Pour into a squeeze bottle.

Balsam fir sauce Heat oil in a saucepan over medium heat. Add onion and garlic and sauté for 5 minutes, until onion is softened. Add salt. Stir in solids from quince-infused whisky and sugar and cook for 8 minutes, until quince is softened.

Pour in wine and reduce by half. Pour in stock and very gently simmer for 20 minutes. Add salal berry juice and verjus.

Transfer to a high-powered blender and blitz until smooth. Pass through a fine-mesh strainer.

Return sauce to the saucepan and bring back to a simmer. Stir in balsam fir and set aside for 10 minutes. Strain. Season with salt and verjus.

Transfer the mixture to a high-powered blender, add Ultratex and blitz again on medium speed for 3 minutes. Pass through a fine-mesh strainer.

Crispy parsnip skins

Sunflower oil, for frying
Reserved parsnip peels from Caramelized Parsnip Purée (see here)

Charred rapini

(100%) 50 g miso
(100%) 50 g water
6 rapini, blanched
(100%) 50 g sunflower oil
(66%) 33 g apple cider vinegar
Salt, to season
Toasted hemp hearts, for sprinkling

Plating

Sunflower oil, for frying
Butter, for basting

Crispy parsnip skins Heat oil in a fryer to 135°C (275°F). Carefully lower peels into the hot oil and fry for 3 minutes, until golden brown.

Crispy parsnip skins can be stored in an airtight container covered by a paper towel for up to 5 days.

Charred rapini Preheat a Konro grill.

In a bowl, combine miso and water and mix well. Glaze rapini with miso paste and grill for 5 minutes, occasionally brushing with more paste, until slightly charred.

Combine oil and vinegar in a bowl. Add rapini and toss to dress. Season with salt and sprinkle with toasted hemp hearts.

Plating Preheat oven to 200°C (400°F).

Heat a little oil in a frying pan over medium heat. Add pavé and sear on all sides. Work in batches, if necessary, to avoid overcrowding. Transfer pavé to a baking sheet, then bake for 10 minutes, until heated through. Place rapini on the baking sheet with pavé to keep warm.

Heat more oil in another frying pan over medium-high heat. Add roulade slices and sear for 5 minutes, until golden. Add 30 g of butter, flip slices over and baste. Sear for another 3 minutes. If needed, finish in the oven with the pavé until heated through.

Arrange dots of purée in the centre of each plate. Place pavé to the left of the dots, then rapini to the right. Overlap three roulade slices of rabbit on top. Add 5 dots of purée around and on the roulade. Garnish with crispy parsnip skins, then pour sauce between rabbit and rapini.

Ferme Rêveuse

It was important for me to find good-quality eggs from a farm that raises their birds with integrity and passion. The conditions of farmed chickens are typically one of the worst, whereby chickens are normally cramped into cages with multiple birds and little room to roam (usually, the space equivalent of a standard sheet of paper). Often, these birds are in such bad shape that they have what are essentially acid burns on their feet and legs from standing in their own droppings for extended periods. High-quality eggs from well-raised chickens may be significantly more expensive than their factory-raised counterparts (costing at least three times more), but I have peace of mind of knowing that the welfare standards for well-raised chickens are higher.

In 2019, I was invited to visit one of the leading chicken farms in the province, if not the country. Even so, this farm wasn't something I wanted to be a part of. Chickens were still kept four to a battery cage. (They're allowed to be up to ten by government regulations, in a measly 51- × 61-cm cage.) They were also cages stacked on top of each other, several metres high, and with no exposure to natural daylight.

Luckily, I found Ferme Rêveuse, a small, family-owned farm that truly cares for their animals. In the summer months, the hens are on pasture in an enriched enclosure that is moved to new grass daily, ensuring lots of food and mental stimulation to keep the birds happy and healthy. The difference between these birds and the ones seen at most chicken farms is night and day. The birds at Ferme Rêveuse are incredibly playful and curious; when I entered the pens, they wanted to interact with me, and they have plenty of access to perches and toys.

During the colder months when it's too frigid for the chickens to thrive outside, they are moved into large barns with heated floors and strong air purification systems. This is the best possible indoor environment for the chickens. They also have plenty of hay and, again, perches and toys to enrich their lives.

It's a pleasure to use eggs from chickens that are so well cared for. Kornel and Olga Schneider are always looking to improve their animals' lives by incorporating "Old World" practices which are better for the animals than the "new age" farming techniques being used. They also sell meat chickens and have started looking into other small animals.

Duck and Beet

When I was eleven years old, my Baba prepared a whole goose for Christmas dinner. I remember the dish perfectly, mainly because I found it to be too aggressive with sauerkraut and wine. (Don't tell Baba.)

This dish was the final savoury course of our opening menu. I wanted to pay homage to the incredible food my Baba makes and to the one dish that I once disliked but now encompasses all my favourite things.

Pickled red pearl onions

(100%) 200 g white wine vinegar
(50%) 100 g water
(25%) 50 g sugar
(5%) 10 g red beet trim
6 pearl onions, petals separated

Duck breast

1 large duck breast
Shio Koji (page 176), to generously coat
Seaweed, soaked
Salt, to season

Sauerkraut croquette

(100%) 500 g sauerkraut, well drained
(10%) 50 g eggs
All-purpose flour, for breading
Egg, beaten, for breading
Panko breadcrumbs, for breading

Beet purée

(100%) 500 g beet, diced
(15%) 75 g melted butter
(1.65%) 8 g salt
(0.5%) 2.5 g baking soda

Pickled red pearl onions In a saucepan, combine all ingredients except onions. Bring to a boil, then set aside to steep for 20 minutes until the liquid is red. Strain through a fine-mesh strainer.

Place onions in a bowl.

In the same saucepan, reheat the liquid to a simmer. Pour the hot mixture over onions, then set aside to cool. Refrigerate for at least 24 hours to pickle.

Duck breast Clean duck breast: remove sinew and clean up skin and edges. Reserve the tender for another use. Place duck in a bowl, then coat in shio koji. Refrigerate for 4 hours.

Wrap duck in seaweed. Leave at room temperature for 30 minutes.

Put duck in a Cook and Hold oven at 60°C (140°F) for at least 2 hours.

Preheat a grill.

Place duck on a clean work surface. Remove seaweed, reserving it for another use. Season duck with salt, then place on the grill. Sear, skin side down, until skin is crispy. Turn, then cook for a minute, until very lightly charred with a smoky depth.

Sauerkraut croquette Line a tray with plastic wrap.

Combine sauerkraut and eggs in a bowl and mix well. Pack the sauerkraut mixture onto the prepared tray, compacting as much as possible. Place in the freezer until frozen but still possible to cut through.

Cut out 5- × 1.2-cm (2- × ½-inch) bars. Freeze for another 30 minutes until fully frozen.

Set up a breading station with flour, egg and panko. Bread croquettes and refrigerate until needed.

Beet purée Note: To create enough pressure in the pressure cooker, this subrecipe makes more than required.

Combine all ingredients in a pressure cooker. Cook on high for 50 minutes. Force release.

Transfer to a high-powered blender and blitz. Pass through a fine-mesh strainer.

Red wine sauce

Sunflower oil, for frying
(100%) 250 g onion
(7%) 18 g garlic
(3%) 8 g tomato paste
(50%) 125 g red wine
(150%) 375 g duck stock
(40%) 100 g Seaweed Water (page 175)
(17%) 42.5 g mirin
(6.5%) 16 g shoyu
(3%) 8 g Ultratex 3

Caramelized salsify

3 salsifies, cut into 3-cm (1¼-inch) segments
(100%) 50 g brown butter
(15%) 8 g miso
(1%) 0.5 g salt

Charred scallions

6 scallions

Plating

Sunflower or canola oil, for deep-frying
Salt, to season
Sunflower shoots
Smoked sea salt, for sprinkling
Lacto-Koji Water (page 176), to season

Red wine sauce Heat oil in a frying pan over medium-high heat. Add onion and garlic and sauté for 7 minutes, until translucent. Add tomato paste and cook for 10 minutes.

Pour in wine, then gently simmer for 5 minutes. Add stock, seaweed water, mirin and shoyu. Gently simmer for 15 minutes.

Transfer to a high-powered blender and blitz. Strain through a fine-mesh strainer.

Return the mixture to the blender, add Ultratex and blend again. Strain through a fine-mesh strainer. Keep warm.

Caramelized salsify Keep salsifies in acidulated water until ready to cook. (We combine 50 g verjus to 1 kg water at the restaurant, but it's not a hard-and-fast ratio. You just want to prevent the salsifies from oxidizing if they're being held for a length of time.)

Add brown butter to a frying pan over medium heat. Add miso and drained salsifies and sauté for 8 minutes, until salsifies can be pierced with a cake tester and still have a slight resistance. Season with salt.

Charred scallion Char scallions with a kitchen torch or on a grill.

Plating Heat oil in a deep fryer or deep saucepan over medium-high heat until it reaches 175°C (347°F). Working in batches to avoid overcrowding, carefully lower the sauerkraut croquettes into the hot oil and deep-fry for 5 minutes, until golden. Using a slotted spoon, transfer the croquettes to a paper towel–lined plate to drain. Season with salt. Repeat with the remaining croquettes.

Using a spoon, swipe beet purée across each serving plate. Arrange salsifies, croquettes, scallions, sunflower shoots and red onions in a row over purée.

Slice duck to your desired size. Season with smoked sea salt and lacto-koji water and arrange next to the purée.

Pour sauce between duck and vegetables and serve immediately.

Duck and Beet, p.78

Goose Heart Raviolo, p.82

Goose Heart Raviolo

I never expected for this dish to remind me of my grandma's tourtière, the one she had made when I was a kid. But by the time I completed the R&D on the filling, this recipe really took me back to those meals.

This version has more complexity, depth of flavour and umami, but it still gives me the same comfort and nostalgia. Guests often comment on how much they love it, even though it sounds and looks so "simple." As with all our pastas, this one is over-sauced so that we can drop off fresh-milled sourdough when the guest is halfway through eating—this way, they have a vehicle for all the extra sauce. This always goes over well.

Alder cure

(100%) 100 g sugar
(100%) 100 g salt
(5%) 5 g alder catkin, toasted

Goose heart filling

(100%) 500 g goose heart
Alder Cure (see here)
(50%) 250 g mushroom trim or any meaty mushroom
Sunflower oil, for frying
(22%) 110 g shallot, sliced
(2%) 10 g garlic, sliced
(1%) 5 g salt, plus extra to season
(10%) 50 g white wine
(5%) 25 g birch syrup
(2%) 10 g miso

Pasta dough

(100%) 500 g all-purpose flour, plus extra for dusting
(56%) 280 g eggs
(7%) 35 g egg yolks
(2.5%) 13 g sunflower oil
Pinch of salt

Raviolo

Pasta Dough (see here)
Goose Heart Filling (see here)
Semolina, for dusting

Alder cure Combine all ingredients in a food processor or Thermomix and blend until uniform.

Goose heart filling Brine goose heart in an 8% salt brine for 45 minutes.

Using a slotted spoon, transfer goose heart to a cutting board. Clean up the top, then slice in half lengthwise. In a bowl, combine heart and alder cure and cure for 4–6 hours.

Using a medium disc on a meat grinder, grind heart. Repeat with mushroom.

Heat oil in a small frying pan over medium heat. Add shallot and garlic, season with salt and sauté until shallot is translucent. Pour in wine, birch syrup and miso and cook until nearly dry *(au sec)*. Add mushroom and cook, uncovered, for 10 minutes, until the excess water from mushroom has evaporated. Add goose heart and cook until just cooked through. Season to taste.

Transfer filling to a bowl and place plastic wrap on filling. Refrigerate overnight.

Mince in a food processor.

Pasta dough Combine all ingredients in an Ankarsrum. (Alternatively, use a stand mixer fitted with the appropriate attachment.) Mix until the dough starts to come together.

Transfer the dough to a clean work surface lightly dusted with flour, then knead the dough to create a strong gluten structure.

Tightly wrap the dough in plastic wrap. Set aside at room temperature for 3 hours or refrigerate overnight. Bring to room temperature before rolling out.

Raviolo Roll out the dough through a pasta roller on the largest setting. Repeat at each setting until just before you reach the thinnest setting. Using a 7-cm (2¾-inch) round cookie cutter, cut out rounds of pasta.

Place 30 g of goose heart filling in the centre of each round of pasta. Gently wet the rim of the pasta with water, then place another round of pasta on top. Crimp the side tightly to seal, pushing out any air bubbles.

Place raviolo on a tray with semolina, then cover with a dish towel until needed.

Ramp and cauliflower purée

(100%) 100 g cauliflower, cut into pieces (include both stem and florets)
(220%) 220 g milk
(9%) 9 g cold butter, cubed
(10%) 10 g ramp greens

Cheese foam

(100%) 200 g reserved cauliflower milk from Ramp and Cauliflower Purée (see here)
(1%) 2 g mustard powder
(1%) 2 g salt
(28%) 56 g Tania Sheep Milk Cheese, shaved

Toasted bee pollen

(100%) 50 g bee pollen

Plating

Fresh-Milled Sourdough Loaf (page 32), to serve

Ramp and cauliflower purée In a saucepan, combine cauliflower and enough milk to cover it. Cook over medium heat for 5–7 minutes, until cauliflower has softened. Drain cauliflower, reserving the cauliflower milk. Set aside 17 g (17%) of milk for use in the purée, reserving the remainder for the cheese foam.

Combine all ingredients in a high-powered blender. Blitz until smooth. Pass through a fine-mesh strainer.

Cheese foam Combine all ingredients except cheese in a Thermomix. Blend on speed 2.5 at 80°C (175°F). Add cheese, a little at a time, then cook for 3–5 minutes, until smooth. Strain through a fine-mesh strainer.

Pour the mixture into an insulated siphon and charge with one N2O charger.

Toasted bee pollen Preheat oven to 175°C (347°F). Line a baking sheet with a Silpat®.

Place bee pollen on the prepared baking sheet. Toast in the oven for 3 minutes, then mix with a spatula. Repeat until bee pollen is dark blonde.

Plating Bring a large pot of salted water to a boil. Carefully lower pasta into the boiling water and cook for 6 minutes.

Place a spoon of purée in a bowl. Using a slotted spoon, place a raviolo on purée. Smother raviolo with cheese foam. Sprinkle with toasted bee pollen.

Serve with sourdough loaf to sop up any leftover sauce.

Beef Heart

When I was devising our opening menu at Perch, I was reluctant to have large animals on it; typically, smaller mammals, poultry and seafood are easier for me to verify in terms of the way the animals are raised, treated and slaughtered.

Since moving to Ottawa, I've worked with Enright Cattle Co. quite a bit and wanted to continue supporting them. And since people love tartare, I decided to showcase the rarely used cut of beef heart to help with whole animal sales. Heart also has a slightly gamier taste, which I love, and the addition of charred bits to a tartare gives the raw meat a much more complex flavour profile. One of the best parts about doing a blind-tasting menu is surprising people with unexpected ingredients. The shock and disbelief when I explain the tartare is made from heart is a fun part of service—and even better when a guest tells me that they loved being out of their comfort zone.

XO sauce

(100%) 50 g pork belly, brunoise
(26%) 13 g garlic, microplaned
(26%) 13 g ginger, brunoise
(43%) 22 g tomato paste
(35%) 18 g dried scallop, reconstituted and minced with a Thermomix
(17%) 9 g dried shrimp, reconstituted and minced with a Thermomix
(11%) 6 g gochujang
(175%) 88 g sunflower oil

Beef heart

(100%) 250 g beef heart, cleaned
(8%) 20 g salt water (8% salinity)

Smoked mayo

(100%) 36 g egg yolks
(70%) 25 g Dijon mustard
(83%) 30 g rice wine vinegar
(1.5%) 0.5 g salt, plus extra to season
(2080%) 749 g canola oil

Roasted peanuts

(100%) 75 g peanuts

Mixed greens

(100%) 100 g rice vinegar
(75%) 75 g sunflower oil
Pinch of salt
(250%) 250 g mixed greens

Plating

(100%) 250 g Beef Heart (see here)
(53%) 133 g XO Sauce solids (see here)
(3%) 8 g XO Sauce liquid (see here)
(13%) 33 g Roasted Peanuts (see here)
(1.3%) 3.3 g salt
Togarashi, for dusting
Tangerine Gem marigold petals, for garnish

XO sauce Fry pork belly in a frying pan over medium-high heat until it starts to crisp. Add garlic and ginger and sauté for 5 minutes. Add tomato paste and stir for 3 minutes. Add scallop, shrimp, gochujang and oil. Simmer on low heat for at least 1 hour, stirring occasionally, taking care not to burn sauce.

Strain, then set aside to cool. Reserve the liquid and solids.

Leftover sauce can be stored in the fridge for 1 week.

Beef heart Combine both ingredients in a bowl. Set aside to brine in the fridge for 45 minutes.

Preheat a Konro grill.

Transfer heart to a cutting board. Slice into steaks, about 2.5-cm (1-inch) thick. Place steaks on the Konro and char each side until darkened, keeping the interior raw. Transfer to a cutting board, then dice.

Smoked mayo Combine all ingredients except oil in a Thermomix or high-powered blender. Turn the machine on, then slowly pour in oil. Season to taste.

Place mayo in a container with a lid, pop one corner of the lid up and place the nozzle of a smoking gun in the container. Add smoke. Once the container is filled with smoke, turn off the smoking gun, remove the nozzle and close the lid tightly. Let sit for 5 minutes, then repeat once.

Leftover smoked mayo can be stored in the fridge for up to 5 days.

Roasted peanuts Preheat oven to 190°C (375°F).

Roast peanuts for 8 minutes, until lightly browned. Transfer to a food processor and roughly blitz.

Mixed greens Combine vinegar, oil and salt in a bowl and whisk well.

Place greens in another bowl, dress according to taste and toss to mix.

Plating Combine beef heart, XO sauce solids and liquid, roasted peanuts and salt in a bowl. Mix well.

Using a 7.5-cm (3-inch) ring mould, divide the mixture among 6 plates. Top the tartare with mixed greens, togarashi and a few marigold petals for garnish. Squeeze a large dot of smoked mayo to the side.

Pulled Shank Chawanmushi

This dish was conceived on possibly the coldest day I have experienced in Ottawa. Chawanmushi, a savoury Japanese egg custard, is warming, but I wanted to magnify its effects on this occasion. That's how I came up with this French onion soup vibe to the chawanmushi. This is a perfect bowl of comfort on a cold winter's night!

Pulled shank

Sunflower oil, for searing
1 whole lamb shank
Salt, to season
(41%) 123 g onion, sliced
(7%) 21 g garlic, sliced
(100%) 300 g red wine
(55%) 165 g red vermouth
(43%) 129 g birch syrup
(15%) 45 g miso
(4%) 12 g sugar kelp

"French onion reduction"

(9%) 9 g butter
(45%) 45 g red onion, sliced
(68%) 68 g sweet onion, sliced
(100%) 100 g yellow onion, sliced
(1.5%) 1.5 g garlic, sliced
(3%) 3 g salt
(17%) 17 g sherry
(9%) 9 g dry vermouth
(226%) 226 g meat stock of your choice
1 bay leaf
(1%) 1 g fish sauce
(1%) 1 g apple cider vinegar

Shiitake dashi

(100%) 170 g seaweed and shiitake-infused water
(11%) 19 g mirin
(7%) 12 g soy sauce
(0.6%) 1 g verjus

Shiitake dashi custard

(75%) 131 g eggs
(100%) 175 g Shiitake Dashi (see here)

Pulled shank Heat oil in a pressure cooker on the sear setting. Generously season lamb shank with salt. Add lamb shank to the pressure cooker and sear well on all sides. Transfer to a plate.

Add onion and garlic to the pressure cooker and sauté for 7 minutes, until lightly browned. Deglaze with wine and vermouth. Stir in birch syrup, miso and sugar kelp and simmer for 2 minutes. Add shank and add enough water to cover. Cook on high for 1 hour. Allow pressure cooker to naturally release pressure.

Remove the lid, then set the pressure cooker aside for shank to cool for 30 minutes.

Transfer shank to a plate, then simmer the liquid until reduced to a quarter of its original yield.

Transfer the reduction to a high-powered blender and blitz. Strain the jus.

Shred lamb, then mix it with 42 g of jus.

"French onion reduction" Melt butter in a saucepan over low heat. Add all three types of onion, garlic and salt and sauté for 1 hour, until golden brown.

Add sherry and vermouth. Increase the heat to medium-high, then simmer and reduce by half. Pour in stock, add bay leaf and gently simmer for 20 minutes. Stir in fish sauce and vinegar.

Transfer the reduction to a high-powered blender and blitz until smooth. Pass through a fine-mesh strainer, then set aside to cool.

Shiitake dashi Combine all ingredients in a bowl and mix well. Strain through a fine-mesh strainer.

Shiitake dashi custard In a bowl, whisk eggs, adding shiitake dashi at the same time. Strain.

Crispy shallots

Sunflower oil, for frying
1 shallot, thinly sliced into rings
Cornstarch, for dredging
Salt, to season

Plating

30 g butter
Smoked sea salt, to season
Sour cream, in a squeeze bottle
1 scallion, thinly sliced on the bias
Calendula petals, for garnish

Crispy shallots Heat oil in a deep fryer or deep saucepan to 135°C (275°F).

Toss shallot in cornstarch, tapping away any excess. Carefully lower shallot into the hot oil and fry for 4 minutes, until golden. Using a slotted spoon, transfer shallot to a paper towel–lined plate. Season with salt while shallot is still hot.

If not using shallot immediately, line an airtight container with a paper towel and store shallot until needed.

Plating Preheat a combi oven to 99°C (210°F).

Pour 50 g of custard base each into 6 heatproof bowls. Steam in the combi oven on the top rack for 5½ minutes with full steam, until set with some wiggle to it.

Meanwhile, warm the pulled lamb and butter in a saucepan. Lightly sprinkle smoked sea salt over the chawanmushi.

To serve, pour 25 g of French onion reduction over the custard. Spoon pulled lamb on top, then surround it with dots of sour cream. Top with a pinch of crispy shallots and sliced scallions. Garnish with calendula petals.

 Pulled Shank Chawanmushi, p.86

Squash and Pork Belly

I spent quite a few years of my career focusing on modernist gastronomy. I'm not a fan of the term, but I played a lot with an ingredient's texture, appearance and form in my early years. I no longer make edible puzzle pieces or freeze-dried chai tea cups filled with a bright green meringue, but I still enjoy the modernist techniques sparingly. For this dish, we turned squash trim into a veil to conceal most of the ingredients underneath—essentially, an adult fruit roll-up.

Squash purée

(100%) 250 g squash, seeded and roasted with minimal colour
(0.5%) 1.3 g salt
(8%) 20 g mirin
(56%) 140 g water

Squash veil

(100%) 200 g Squash Purée (see here)
(50%) 100 g isomalt

Roasted squash

Neutral oil, for drizzling
1 kabocha squash, halved lengthwise
Salt, to season

Pumpkin seed emulsion

(100%) 175 g toasted pumpkin seeds
(133%) 233 g water
(10%) 18 g fennel fronds
(12%) 21 g mirin
(13%) 23 g apple cider vinegar
(7.5%) 13 g Dijon mustard
(5%) 9 g sesame oil

Crispy sage

Sunflower oil, for deep-frying
12 sage leaves, stemmed
Salt, to season

Pickled fennel stem

(100%) 200 g white wine vinegar
(50%) 100 g water
(25%) 50 g sugar
1 fennel stem, cut into 3-mm (⅛-inch) thick slices

Plating

450 g pork belly, cut into 6 slices
1 red finger chili, thinly sliced

Squash purée Combine all ingredients in a saucepan and bring to a simmer. Simmer for 12 minutes, until softened without resistance.

Transfer the mixture to a high-powered blender and blend until smooth. Pass through a fine-mesh strainer. Set aside to cool.

Squash veil Combine both ingredients in a saucepan and bring to a simmer. Cook until isomalt is fully dissolved.

Spread out the mixture to a thickness of about 1 mm (1⁄32 inch) on a sheet of acetate. Place in a dehydrator set at 40°C (105°F) for 4 hours. Cut into 10-cm (4-inch) squares.

Roasted squash Preheat oven to 190°C (375°F).

Drizzle oil over squash. Season with salt. Place squash, flesh side down, on a baking sheet and roast for 20 minutes, until tender. (You should be able to insert a cake tester through the thickest part without resistance.) Set aside to cool.

Slice along the ridges to create wedges. Using a paring knife, remove the skin. Cut squash into bite-size pieces. Set aside.

Pumpkin seed emulsion Combine all ingredients in a high-powered blender and blend until smooth. Pass through a fine-mesh strainer.

Crispy sage Heat oil in a deep fryer to 110°C (230°F). Carefully lower sage into the hot oil and deep-fry for 3 minutes, until crispy. Transfer to a paper towel–lined plate to drain. Season with salt.

Leftover crispy sage can be stored in an airtight container lined with a paper towel for up to 5 days.

Pickled fennel stem In a saucepan, combine vinegar, water and sugar. Bring to a boil.

Place fennel in a bowl, then pour the pickling liquid over it. Set aside to cool.

Plating Spread pumpkin seed emulsion in the centre of each plate.

Heat a frying pan over medium-high heat. Add pork belly and sear both sides. Slice into 3 pieces.

Arrange pork belly and roasted squash over pumpkin seed emulsion. Garnish with chili and pickled fennel stem.

Cut out a square squash veil large enough to cover pork belly and squash. Arrange crispy sage on top of the veil.

sea

HYPERLITE

Matane Shrimp Cone with Tartare and Caviar

I love to create one or two bitters because they must hit so many notes. For this one, I wanted venison tartare and caviar to be the main components, but I couldn't work out the ingredients for the cone. We had an excess of frozen Matane shrimp from a past event, and the shrimp's natural sweetness proved to be the perfect companion to the depth of the charred tartare and the brininess of the caviar. The first day we served this course, we had a table of four people who were amused by the playfulness of this dish when it was placed on the table and continued raving about it after eating it. We knew we had something special with this course.

Shio koji–aged venison tartare

1 venison loin, cleaned
Shio Koji (page 176), to coat

Prawn cone

(100%) 75 g raw Matane shrimp
(71%) 53 g egg whites
(68%) 51 g water
(1.5%) 1.1 g sea truffle
(26%) 20 g icing sugar
(3%) 2.3 g salt
(85%) 64 g all-purpose flour

Sea truffle emulsion

(100%) 36 g egg yolks
(7%) 2.5 g mirin
(33%) 12 g balsamic vinegar
(6.5%) 2.3 g sea truffle
(2.5%) 0.9 g salt
(1000%) 360 g sunflower oil, plus extra if needed

Venison and sea truffle

(100%) 100 g Shio Koji–Aged Venison Tartare (see here)
(25%) 25 g Sea Truffle Emulsion (see here)
(14%) 14 g shallot, brunoise
(8%) 8 g venison Garum (page 178)
(1%) 1 g salt

Shrimp garamel

(225%) 113 g sugar
(42%) 21 g water
(17%) 9 g verjus
(100%) 50 g Old Habits Pacific Pink Shrimp garum

Sunflower seeds

Sunflower seeds, toasted

Plating

Crème fraîche
Cornflower petals
Caviar

Shio koji–aged venison tartare Coat venison in shio koji. Refrigerate for 24–48 hours.

Put venison in the freezer for 2 hours.

Heat a frying pan over high heat. Add venison and sear on all sides until charred but raw on the inside. Dice.

Prawn cone Preheat a combi oven to 177°C (350°F).

Combine all ingredients in a high-powered blender and blend until smooth.

Spray a Silpat® baking mat with non-stick spray. Using a cone stencil, spread the mixture on the Silpat®. Bake for 4 minutes with level 2 fan. Set aside to cool.

Gently peel the prawn cone from the Silpat®, then roll it around an ovenproof cone mould. Place the cone with the cone mould on a wire rack set on a baking sheet. Decrease the combi oven to 95°C (203°F) with full fan and bake for 25 minutes, until dried and golden.

Sea truffle emulsion Combine all ingredients except oil in a high-powered blender and blitz until smooth. With the motor running, slowly pour in oil and blend until thickened and emulsified. There should be enough oil in the blender to blitz the sea truffle. If necessary, add a little more oil.

Venison and sea truffle Combine all ingredients in a bowl and mix.

Shrimp garamel In a small saucepan, combine sugar, water and verjus. Bring to a boil, then cook to a caramel. Remove from heat, then slowly and very carefully add garum, as it will splatter.

Sunflower seeds Blitz to a rough consistency.

Plating Dip the top few millimetres of cone into garamel, then roll cone in the ground sunflower seeds. Fill cone with venison and sea truffle. Place a small dot of crème fraîche on top and arrange cornflower petals around the cone. Finish with a spoonful of caviar.

Asparagus and Lobster

This dish was conceptualized after I tasted the lacto-koji and butter sauce from *The NOMA Guide to Fermentation* cookbook. After making the sauce, I had an immediate yet abnormal craving for lobster and asparagus. This dish showcases those three ingredients beautifully and cleanly. They play perfectly when mixed, yet each holds their own to stand out in the dish.

Koji oil

- (100%) 50 g Koji, dried (page 175)
- (250%) 125 g sunflower oil

Cured lobster

- (100%) 100 g salt
- (100%) 100 g sugar
- (24%) 24 g cedar leaves
- 1 lobster, separate lobster tail, claws and legs

Ricotta

- (100%) 1 kg milk
- Pinch of salt
- (2%) 20 g vinegar, such as white vinegar or apple cider vinegar

Charred whey-poached asparagus

- 6 large asparagus
- Reserved whey from Ricotta (see here)

Mayo

- (100%) 36 g egg yolks
- (42%) 15 g rice wine vinegar
- (33%) 12 g Dijon mustard
- (1042%) 375 g canola oil
- Salt, to taste

Koji oil Combine both ingredients in a high-powered blender and blitz on high speed for 6 minutes. Pour the mixture into a container, then refrigerate overnight.

The next day, slightly warm koji oil in a saucepan, stirring continuously to prevent it from burning. Pass the mixture through an oil filter, pressing out as much oil as possible. Pour oil into a squeeze bottle.

Cured lobster In a Thermomix, combine salt, sugar and cedar and blitz.

Bring a pot of salted water to a boil. Cook the lobster parts separately: the tail for 4–6 minutes, claws for 3 minutes and legs for 1 minute. Plunge in an ice bath. When cool enough to handle, remove meat from shells.

Cover lobster meat in the salt mixture, then refrigerate for 45 minutes–1 hour. Rinse lobster well. Pat dry.

Ricotta In a large saucepan, combine milk and salt. Stir over medium heat until the mixture reaches 85°C (185°F). Stir in vinegar until the mixture begins to curdle. Leave untouched, holding the temperature between 79°C and 88°C (174°F and 190°F) for 20 minutes.

Line a perforated hotel pan with cheesecloth. Place it inside a deeper hotel pan. Gently pour the mixture into the cheesecloth. Refrigerate for 20 minutes to drain. Chill until needed. Reserve whey for the whey-poached asparagus.

Charred whey-poached asparagus Peel asparagus, then cut the spears into 2.5-cm (1-inch) segments, leaving the asparagus tips whole.

In a saucepan over medium-high heat, combine cut asparagus segments and tips and whey and poach for 4 minutes, until just cooked. Refrigerate to cool.

Drain asparagus. Separate segments and tips. Char tips with a torch.

Mayo In a Thermomix or high-powered blender, combine egg yolks, vinegar and mustard. With the motor running, slowly add oil and blend until emulsified. Season with salt.

Lobster "salad"	(100%) 100 g Cured Lobster (see here), brunoise (11%) 11 g green apple, brunoise (22%) 22 g Mayo (see here)
Charred jalapeno juice	5 jalapenos
Lacto-koji sauce	(100%) 200 g Lacto-Koji Water (page 176) (50%) 100 g butter, cubed Salt, to taste
Plating	Red vein sorrel, for garnish

Lobster "salad" Combine all ingredients in a bowl and mix well.

Charred jalapeno juice Preheat a Konro grill.

Add jalapenos and sear on all sides until charred. Transfer to a cutting board, then remove stems and seeds.

Place jalapenos in a juicer and juice. Pour into a squeeze bottle.

Lacto-koji sauce Bring lacto-koji water to a simmer in a small saucepan. Whisk in butter, one cube at a time. Season with salt. Keep warm on the stove (do not boil) and whisk occasionally to keep emulsified.

Plating Place 25 g of ricotta on the bottom of each bowl and spread out, pressing against the bowl to create a foundation for asparagus.

Stand asparagus segments in a tight pack into the ricotta foundation. Squeeze a few drops of jalapeno juice on top, depending on your desired spice level. Place a charred asparagus tip on the left side of the segments. Add a quenelle of lobster salad next to it.

Garnish lobster with a red vein sorrel leaf. Pour in 50 g of lacto-koji sauce. Squeeze a few drops of koji oil into sauce.

 Asparagus and Lobster, p.100

Licorice Butter-Poached Crab Chawanmushi, p.104

Licorice Butter–Poached Crab Chawanmushi

Kato in L.A. deserves a shout-out for the inspiration behind this dish. I had one of my best meals ever at the restaurant—the food, atmosphere, service and drinks were all perfectly executed—and they even had a course with a vinegar "sidecar." Diners added the vinegar to suit their taste, and this approach resonated with me. I wanted to bring this idea to Perch; so what better way to incorporate a vinegar that you add yourself than with a chawanmushi?

Charred seaweed vinegar

(100%)	250 g rice wine vinegar
(5%)	13 g sugar kelp, charred
(5%)	13 g macro kelp, charred

Rock crab dashi

(100%)	275 g Seaweed Water (page 175)
(8%)	22 g mirin
(5%)	14 g shoyu
(0.3%)	0.8 g salt
(5%)	14 g rock crab shells, roasted

Rock crab chawanmushi

(75%)	225 g eggs
(100%)	300 g Rock Crab Dashi (see here)

Charred seaweed broth

	Sunflower oil, for frying
(16%)	16 g shallot, sliced
(2%)	2 g garlic, sliced
(1%)	1 g salt
(5%)	5 g miso
(11%)	11 g sake
(25%)	25 g mirin
(2%)	2 g sugar kelp, heavily charred
(1%)	1 g macro kelp, heavily charred
(100%)	100 g Seaweed Water (page 175)

Wild licorice–infused butter

(100%)	100 g butter
(10%)	10 g dehydrated wild licorice root

Charred seaweed vinegar Combine all ingredients in a bowl. Set aside at room temperature for at least 3 weeks. (Because the kelp is submerged in the vinegar and won't go off, there is no maximum time.)

Transfer to a dropper bottle.

Rock crab dashi In a saucepan, combine seaweed water, mirin, shoyu and salt. Bring to a simmer, then add crab shells. Remove from heat, then set aside for 10 minutes. Strain through a fine-mesh strainer.

Rock crab chawanmushi In a bowl, whisk eggs, adding rock crab dashi at the same time. Strain.

Charred seaweed broth Heat oil in a frying pan over medium-high heat. Add shallot, garlic and salt and sauté for 10 minutes, until translucent.

Stir in miso and sake and simmer until reduced by half. Add mirin and simmer for 2 minutes. Stir in both seaweeds and cook for 2 minutes. Pour in seaweed water and very gently simmer for 20 minutes.

Strain through a medium (not fine-mesh) strainer. Reserve the solids and dehydrate for another purpose.

Wild licorice–infused butter Melt butter in a small saucepan over medium heat. Add licorice root and set aside to steep for 10 minutes. Strain.

Green daikon coins

1 green daikon

Plating

Rock crab
Smoked sea salt, to taste
Camelina seeds
Walnut oil, for drizzling
Geranium petals

Green daikon coins Using a mandoline, slice daikon about 5-mm (¼-inch) thick. Using a 1-cm (½-inch) round cutter, cut out small rounds.

Plating Preheat a combi oven to 99°C (210°F).

Clean crab. Pick meat from shells, meticulously ensuring all shells have been removed.

Pour 50 g of chawanmushi base each into 6 heatproof bowls. Steam in the combi oven on the top rack for 5½ minutes with full steam, until set with some wiggle to it.

Meanwhile, in a small saucepan over low heat, poach crab in 50 g of wild licorice–infused butter until warmed through. Drain.

Lightly season chawanmushi with smoked sea salt. Pour 15 mL of charred seaweed broth on top.

Place 25 g of crab in the centre of each bowl of chawanmushi. Sprinkle with camelina seeds, drizzle with walnut oil and top with a few geranium petals. Place 5 daikon coins around the crab.

As you eat, the flavours will mellow out as the dish cools. Add a few drops of charred seaweed vinegar to change the complexity and bring the flavours back to life.

Crab and Pork

This dish is complex, layered and eclectic yet simple to put together—it's all over the map yet feels very familiar. Fogo Island crabs are beautiful, sustainable and sweet in flavour; using the product also helps a small community. The plating is time consuming but gorgeous. Our team loved the flavour and look of this dish, and we were all sad when we removed it from the menu.

Crème fraîche

(100%) 250 g whipping cream
(13%) 33 g buttermilk
(13%) 33 g yogurt

Pork broth

(100%) 1.8 kg pork bones and trim, roasted
(15%) 270 g onion
(13%) 240 g carrot
(8%) 144 g celery
(0.5%) 9 g kombu
(2%) 36 g shiso leaves
(1%) 18 g smoked sea salt

Tomato shrub fluid gel

(100%) 250 g chilled Tomato Shrub (page 177)
(1.2%) 3 g agar-agar

Koji butter

(100%) 100 g butter
(15%) 15 g Koji, dried (page 175)

Fogo Island crab

1 Fogo Island crab

Daikon and kohlrabi

1 purple daikon
1 green daikon
1 giant Prague kohlrabi
Salt, to season

Crème fraîche Combine all ingredients in a bowl and mix. Cover and set aside at room temperature for 3–4 days, until thickened.

In a strainer set over a bowl, place a cheesecloth or oil filter. Pour in crème fraîche and refrigerate overnight to strain.

Pork broth Note: This is the maximum weight of ingredients for a standard-size pressure cooker.

Place pork, onion, carrot, celery and kombu in a pressure cooker. Cook on high for 4 hours. Release pressure naturally.

Strain broth. Add shiso and smoked sea salt. Set aside to cool, then strain again.

Tomato shrub fluid gel In a saucepan, combine both ingredients and mix well. Bring to a simmer, stirring occasionally.

Pour the mixture into a heatproof container. Set aside to cool, then refrigerate until completely solid.

Koji butter Simmer butter in a frying pan. Remove from heat and add koji. Set aside to steep for 10 minutes. Strain.

Fogo Island crab Pick meat from shells, meticulously ensuring all shells have been removed.

Daikon and kohlrabi Using a mandoline, carefully slice both daikons and kohlrabi to a 1-mm (1⁄32-inch) thickness. Cut out vegetables with a 3-cm (1¼-inch) round cookie cutter.

Just before plating, lightly season with salt.

Plating Transfer tomato shrub fluid gel to a high-powered blender and blitz on high speed until smooth. Strain through a fine-mesh strainer.

In a saucepan, warm crab in koji butter. Transfer crab to a paper towel–lined plate to drain. Place 50–60 g in a mound in the centre of each bowl.

Place 8 random dots each of crème fraîche and tomato shrub fluid gel on the crab. Arrange 5 discs of each daikon and kohlrabi on top, using crème fraîche and gel to keep them in place.

In a saucepan, bring pork broth to a light simmer, then gently pour into each bowl.

Grilled Honey Mussels and Tomato Broth

One of my favourite screw-up stories is from C Restaurant when Chef Quang Dang was the chef de cuisine. It was my first time working in fine dining. I had no idea what I was doing and I was so nervous, but I had the drive to push forward. It was a small team, and for some wild reason, they trusted me at the fish station and threw me into the proverbial fire! Honey Mussels were on the menu, and at that time, being from the prairies, I didn't know that was a mussel variety. So I assumed I had to add honey to the mussels while they cooked. . . I was wrong! It went unnoticed for weeks until one busy service when Chef Quang Dang looked over to see me pouring honey into the pan of mussels. When the chef asked me what I was doing and I said, "Honey mussels," his expression was priceless. I felt like an idiot.

After what felt like an eternity, chef said it didn't really matter since it was probably "f*&%ing delicious" but to stop doing it—and ask questions if I wasn't positive on something. The point of that story (aside from the fact that I love sharing it) is that C Restaurant gave me an appreciation for seafood and, more so, for Honey Mussels from the West Coast!

Kombu oil

(6%) 12 g kombu, soaked until pliable
(100%) 200 g sunflower oil

Grilled Honey Mussels

Live Honey Mussels
Kombu Oil (see here)

Grilled tomato and dulse broth

(100%) 225 g grilled tomato, roughly chopped
(73%) 164 g water
(2.5%) 6 g dulse
(1.5%) 3.4 g gochujang
(7%) 16 g verjus
(9%) 20 g mirin
(0.03%) 0.07 g bay leaf (to the nearest amount of bay leaf, probably 1 or 2)
(3.9%) 9 g salt

Oyster pudding

(100%) 125 g oyster meat with juice
(333%) 416 g whipping cream
(10%) 13 g sugar
(1% of above total weight) ~5.5 g agar-agar
(29%) 36 g egg yolks

Kombu oil Preheat a Konro grill.

Add kombu and grill until lightly charred.

In a saucepan, combine oil and kombu and heat to 100°C (212°F). Set aside to cool to 64°C (147°F). Strain, then hold at that temperature.

Grilled Honey Mussels Preheat a Konro grill.

Place mussels in a bowl and run cold water over them for 20 minutes. Drain, then remove dirt.

Grill mussels for 8–12 minutes. Remove mussels from shells. Remove beards. Place in the heated kombu oil (64°C/147°F).

Refrigerate to cool, ensuring mussels are completely submerged for at least 24 hours.

Mussels can be stored in the fridge for up to 7 days.

Grilled tomato and dulse broth In a pressure cooker, combine all ingredients except salt. Cook on high for 40 minutes. Release pressure naturally.

Strain through a Superbag or oil filter. Place the solids in a dehydrator set at 60°C (140°F) until dried.

In a high-powered blender that is completely dry, blend the solids on high until powdered. Reserve.

Whisk salt into the liquid.

Oyster pudding In a Thermomix, combine all ingredients except egg yolks. Bring to 95°C (203°F). Cool down to 60°C (140°F). Blitz in egg yolks. Remove from heat, then refrigerate to cool and harden.

Return the mixture to the Thermomix and blitz again. Strain, then pour into a bottle.

Sautéed Tokyo turnip greens		Tokyo turnip greens
Sea truffle butter	(100%)	150 g butter, melted
	(1.5%)	2.3 g sea truffle seaweed, ground with a spice grinder
Tokyo turnip coins		3–4 Tokyo turnips
Pickled sea asparagus	(100%)	225 g rice wine vinegar
	(50%)	113 g water
	(25%)	56 g sugar
		30 sea asparagus, trimmed
Plating		Salt, to season
		Fennel pollen, to season
		Geranium petals, for garnish

Sautéed Tokyo turnip greens Remove greens from bulbs.

Bring a saucepan of salted water to a boil. Add greens and blanch until wilted. Drain, then set aside to cool slightly. Cut into 5-mm (¼-inch) lengths.

Sea truffle butter Combine both ingredients in a saucepan. Heat butter to 50°C (122°F) and hold at that temperature for 5 minutes. Set aside to cool and harden.

Tokyo turnip coins Using a mandoline, slice turnips about 2-mm (1⁄16-inch) thick. Using a 2.5-cm (1-inch) ring mould, cut out discs from the slices.

Pickled sea asparagus In a saucepan, combine vinegar, water and sugar and bring to a simmer. Place sea asparagus in a bowl and pour the mixture over the asparagus.

Plating In a saucepan over medium heat, sauté turnip greens in 30 g of sea truffle butter until cooked and wilted. Season with a pinch of salt. Add sea asparagus and sauté for another 30 seconds. Transfer greens to a paper towel–lined plate to drain.

In another saucepan over medium heat, reheat broth.

Place 30 g of turnip greens in each bowl. Add 5 sea asparagus to each, then top with mussels. Season with fennel pollen and reserved broth solids.

Squeeze 9 dots of oyster pudding on mussels. Rest turnip coins on mussels. Garnish with geranium petals. Pour in broth beside mussels.

Grilled Honey Mussels and Tomato Broth, p.108

Octopus and Burnt Onion, p.112

Octopus and Burnt Onion

When working with great suppliers who share our ethics, we sometimes create dishes around their recommendations of products. Organic Ocean in British Columbia had an excess of octopuses and suggested we use them because they could guarantee a steady number of beautiful octopus. We came up with this dish. It doesn't hurt that octopus is delicious and has a beautiful texture when done well.

Kvass reduction

- (15%) 150 g fresh or stale bread (we prefer stale to minimize food waste), coarsely chopped
- (100%) 1 kg hot water (77°C/170°F)

Kvass fermentation

- 100% Kvass Reduction (see here)
- 1% active sourdough starter
- 5% honey

Burnt onion juice

- Sunflower oil, for roasting
- (100%) 500 g yellow onion, quartered

Burnt onion reduction

- (100%) 225 g reserved liquid from Burnt Onion Juice (see here)
- (6%) 14 g mirin

Octopus

- Octopus
- Salt, to cover
- (100%) 500 g reserved pulp from Burnt Onion Juice (see here)
- (28%) 140 g mirin
- (20%) 100 g verjus
- Poultry stock, to cover
- (2%) 10 g kombu

Kvass reduction Preheat oven to 175°C (347°F) with 100% fan.

Place bread on a baking sheet and bake for 6 minutes. Transfer bread to a large heatproof jar, then add water. Cover and set aside for 8–24 hours.

Strain through cheesecloth, wringing out as much liquid as possible. Reserve the liquid.

Kvass fermentation Note: Because this subrecipe will never make the same amount, weight measurements are not included.

Combine all ingredients in a large fermentation jar that's fitted with an airlock. Stir. Seal the jar. Set aside at room temperature for 3 days.

Strain through cheesecloth, then place in a half hotel pan. Place the hotel pan in a dehydrator set at 60°C (140°F) and reduce to a quarter of the original amount.

Burnt onion juice Preheat oven to 220°C (425°F).

Preheat an ovenproof frying pan over high heat. Add enough oil to coat the bottom of the pan. Add onion and char well on all sides.

Place the pan in the oven and roast onion for 15 minutes, until softened. Set aside to cool.

Juice onion, reserving pulp for later use.

Burnt onion reduction Combine both ingredients in a saucepan and simmer until reduced to 40% of their original weight (~96 g).

Octopus Note: The quantities for this subrecipe are designed to fill a standard pressure cooker. Do not scale up; otherwise, the mixture will overflow.

Separate tentacles, then place in a large bowl. Rub salt over them to help remove impurities. Rinse under cold running water.

Combine all ingredients in a pressure cooker. Cook on high for 13 minutes. Release pressure naturally. Set aside to cool for about 30 minutes.

Remove octopus head and reserve for garum (page 178). Transfer tentacles to a chopping board and cut into 10-cm (4-inch) lengths or your desired size.

Strain the liquid from the remaining pressure cooker mixture, reserving both the liquid and solids.

Burnt pearl onions	3 white pearl onions, tips and tails
Burnt onion purée	(100%) 100 g reserved solids from Octopus (see here) (25%) 25 g reserved pulp from Burnt Onion Juice (see here) (25%) 25 g reserved liquid from Octopus (see here) (10%) 10 g miso (4%) 4 g Snail Garamel (page 54) or Shrimp Garamel (page 96) (0.3%) 0.3 g aji charapita pepper Ultratex 3
Rutabaga confit	500 g rutabaga Salt
Squash brunoise	(37.5%) 75 g brown butter (100%) 200 g koginut squash, brunoise
Squash and onion mix	(100%) 125 g Squash Brunoise (see here) (30%) 38 g Burnt Onion Reduction (see here) (4%) 5 g balsamic vinegar (0.8%) 1 g salt
Nasturtium oil	(100%) 75 g nasturtium greens (500%) 375 g sunflower oil
Plating	Pinch of salt Nasturtium leaves, for garnish

Burnt pearl onions Halve onions lengthwise. Remove skins. Place onions on a rack set over a tray. Torch the cut side of onions, then set aside to cool. Separate petals, reserving 12.

Burnt onion purée In a high-powered blender, combine all ingredients except Ultratex and blitz until smooth. Add Ultratex 1 g at a time and blitz until the mixture is thick enough to mound slightly on a spoon. Pass through a fine-mesh strainer.

Rutabaga confit Juice rutabaga, reserving pulp. Make note of the separate weights of the juice and solids.

Slowly simmer rutabaga juice in a saucepan over medium heat until liquid measures 16% of its original weight.

In a bowl, mix reserved pulp (100%) with 66% of reduced juice and 4% salt.

Squash brunoise Heat brown butter in a frying pan over medium heat. Add squash and sauté for 4 minutes, until cooked with a bit of bite.

Squash and onion mix Mix all ingredients in a bowl.

Nasturtium oil Bring a small saucepan of water to a boil. Add nasturtium greens and blanch. Plunge in an ice bath.

Once cooled, combine greens and oil in a high-powered blender and blitz until entirely incorporated. Strain through an oil filter.

Plating Preheat a Konro grill.

Skewer octopus and grill for 6 minutes, rotating and brushing with the kvass fermentation. Remove from heat, then season with salt.

Place rutabaga confit on the far-left side of each plate. Top with octopus. To the right of the octopus, spoon a dollop of burnt onion purée and garnish with a couple of nasturtium leaves. To the right of the burnt onion purée, place a quenelle of squash and onion mix. Place 2 charred pearl onion petals around the squash and onion mix and fill them with nasturtium oil.

Pike Agnolotti Pasta

I once prepared an eel mousse dish where the eel was marinated in a traditional unagi sauce. I wanted to do something similar at Perch using only Canadian ingredients.

Finding eel in Canada is no easy task. One day, my friends at Affinity Fish mentioned they had a huge northern pike aging in their fridge—it seemed like the perfect fish for this technique. As a kid, I used to fish for walleye with my grandpa. Every time we caught a pike, he would release it immediately without question because of their annoying bone structure. Eels also have a unique bone structure, so it seemed fitting to use pike for the mousse filling in the agnolotti.

Roasted birch-marinated pike

(100%) 200 g shoyu
(95%) 190 g mirin
(13%) 26 g molasses
(9%) 18 g birch syrup
1 pike fillet

Crispy king oyster mushroom

1 king oyster mushroom
Reserved marinade from Roasted Birch-Marinated Pike (see here), for brushing

Pasta dough

(100%) 500 g all-purpose flour, plus extra for dusting
(81.6%) 408 g eggs
(7.2%) 36 g egg yolks
(2.6%) 13 g camelina oil
Pinch of salt

Charred eggplant purée

(100%) 225 g eggplant
Sunflower oil, for frying
(25%) 56 g shallot, thinly sliced
(5%) 11 g garlic, sliced
Salt, to season
(5%) 11 g tomato paste
(5%) 11 g brown anchovies
(2.2%) 5 g balsamic vinegar
(0.9%) 2 g salt

Roasted potato

2 large russet potatoes

Roasted birch-marinated pike On a tray, combine all ingredients except pike. Mix well, then add pike and marinate in the fridge for 24 hours.

Preheat oven to 205°C (401°F).

Transfer pike to a sheet of aluminum foil, reserving marinade. Place on a baking sheet and bake for 15 minutes, until the fish is flaky but not mushy. Set aside until cool enough to handle.

Flake meat from skin, carefully removing bones.

Crispy king oyster mushroom Slice mushroom on a mandoline, about 1.5-mm (1/24-inch) thick. Brush marinade on both sides of mushroom and place on a sheet of acetate. Place in a dehydrator set at 40°C (105°F) for 24 hours.

Pasta dough Combine all ingredients in an Ankarsrum. (Alternatively, use a stand mixer fitted with the appropriate attachment.)

Transfer to a work counter lightly dusted with flour. With lightly wet hands, finish kneading until the dough comes together. Wrap tightly in plastic wrap, then set aside at room temperature for at least 3 hours, or overnight in the fridge. Bring to room temperature before rolling out.

Charred eggplant purée Preheat oven to 205°C (401°F). Also, preheat a Konro grill.

Place eggplant on the grill and char until soft. Transfer eggplant to the oven and bake for another 12 minutes, until very soft. Set aside until cool enough to handle, then remove flesh from skin.

Heat oil in a small frying pan over low heat. Add shallot and garlic and sauté for 10 minutes, until translucent. You want to take your time to build flavour. Season with a pinch of salt. Add tomato paste and anchovies and cook for another 10 minutes. Add eggplant and cook for another 5 minutes, until completely broken down.

Transfer the mixture to a high-powered blender. Add vinegar and salt and blend until smooth. Pass through a fine-mesh strainer, then set aside to cool.

Roasted potato Preheat oven to 205°C (401°F).

Pierce potatoes with a fork and bake for 25 minutes, until softened. Set aside until cool enough to handle. Remove skins.

Pike mousse

- (100%) 300 g Roasted Birch-Marinated Pike (see here)
- (50%) 150 g Roasted Potato (see here)
- (37.5%) 113 g reserved marinade from Roasted Birch-Marinated Pike (see here)
- Salt, to taste

Pike agnolotti

- Pasta Dough (see here)
- Pike Mousse (see here)
- Semolina, for sprinkling

Reduction

- (100%) 450 g rice wine vinegar
- (15%) 68 g shallot, sliced
- (5%) 23 g garlic, sliced
- (3%) 14 g ginger, sliced
- (3%) 14 g dulse

Seaweed beurre blanc

- (85%) 191 g sake
- (57%) 128 g Reduction (see here)
- (100%) 225 g chilled butter, cubed
- Splash of whipping cream (optional)
- Salt, to season

Kombu powder

- (100%) 20 g dried kombu

Plating

- Sunflower oil, for tossing
- Micro shungiku, for garnish

Pike mousse Combine all ingredients except salt in an Ankarsrum. (Alternatively, use a stand mixer fitted with the appropriate attachment.) Mix well. Season with salt. Transfer the mixture to a piping bag.

Pike agnolotti Roll out the dough through a pasta roller, starting at the largest setting, then working your way down to the second thinnest (or to your desired thickness). Pipe the mousse, about 2 cm (¾ inch) away from the edge, along the length of the pasta. Roll the pasta over the filling to cover, then trim excess dough. Pinch the tube of pasta at 5-cm (2-inch) intervals to seal. Using a cutter, cut agnolotti.

Sprinkle semolina onto a tray. Add the prepared agnolotti and cover with a dish towel until needed.

Reduction Combine all ingredients in a saucepan. Simmer until reduced to a third of the original amount.

Seaweed beurre blanc In a saucepan or Thermomix, combine sake and reduction. Simmer until reduced by half. Lower temperature slightly.

Whisk in butter, one cube at a time, allowing butter to melt after each addition. Do not stop whisking. If needed, add cream to help emulsify. Season to taste with salt. (The reduction solids from the beurre blanc can be dehydrated for use in Broccoli and Sea Buckthorn [page 46].)

Kombu powder Blitz dried kombu, then pass through a strainer (not fine mesh).

Plating Bring a pot of water to a boil. Carefully lower agnolotti into the boiling water and cook for 5 minutes, working in batches, if necessary, to avoid overcrowding.

Using a slotted spoon, transfer agnolotti to a bowl. Gently toss with a little oil.

Place pasta in each bowl. Squeeze dots of charred eggplant purée on pasta and dust with kombu powder. Arrange 3 mushroom slices and a little mound of shungiku on top. Pour beurre blanc into the bowl.

Pike Agnolotti Pasta, p.114

Rose-Cured Spot Prawns, p.118

Rose-Cured Spot Prawns

Spot prawn season in Canada is a big deal, especially out West—so much so that the Chefs' Table Society of British Columbia hosts an annual spot prawn festival in the Vancouver neighbourhood of False Creek.

When I visited Golden Eagle Black Cod on Salt Spring Island (page 138), we dropped a few spot prawn traps in the area. We caught enough for each of us to have a handful and ate them raw only a few minutes after pulling them out of the water—it is truly an incredible experience.

While we can't give that experience at the restaurant, we can still prepare a nice expression of spot prawn. The West is home to the beautiful Nootka rose, which has a unique, mildly bitter flavour that complements fresh spot prawns. If you can't find that rose variety, any wild rose will do.

Crème fraîche

(100%) 250 g whipping cream
(13%) 33 g buttermilk
(13%) 33 g yogurt

Roasted spot prawn broth: part 1

(100%) 153 g spot prawn heads and shells, well rinsed
(9.8%) 15 g pineappleweed greens
(81%) 124 g Koji, dried (page 175)
(4.2%) 6 g kelp
(81.7%) 125 g rhubarb stalks, roughly chopped
(9.8%) 15 g honey, blackened in a black garlic fermenter
(1557%) 2382 g filtered water

Roasted spot prawn broth: part 2

100% Roasted Spot Prawn Broth: Part 1 (see here)
1.7% salt
10% verjus
15% Kohlrabi Shrub (page 177)
0.25% of above total weight agar-agar

Rose cure

(420%) 168 g sugar
(210%) 84 g salt
(100%) 40 g fresh rose petals

Rose-cured spot prawns

(100%) 18 spot prawns, cleaned
Rose Cure (see here), to coat

Crème fraîche Combine all ingredients in a lidded container. Mix well, then set aside at room temperature for 3–4 days, until thickened.

Line a strainer with cheesecloth or an oil filter and set over a bowl. Place crème fraîche in the strainer and refrigerate overnight to drain.

Roasted spot prawn broth: part 1 Note: The quantities for this subrecipe are designed to fill a standard pressure cooker. Do not scale up; otherwise, the mixture will overflow.

Preheat oven to 220°C (425°F).

Place spot prawns on a baking sheet and roast for 8 minutes.

Combine all ingredients in a pressure cooker. Cook on high for 45 minutes. Release pressure naturally. Strain.

Roasted spot prawn broth: part 2 Combine all ingredients in a saucepan over medium heat and heat until the mixture starts to simmer. Set aside to cool. Refrigerate overnight.

Set a perforated pan over a hotel pan and line the perforated pan with cheesecloth. Whisk the slightly set prawn broth to break it up, then pour it over the cheesecloth. Set aside to rest at room temperature overnight, as the liquid will slowly separate from the solids through the cheesecloth, creating a clear consommé of prawn broth.

Rose cure Combine all ingredients in a high-powered blender, Thermomix or food processor and blitz.

Rose-cured spot prawns Coat spot prawns in rose cure. Set aside for 40 minutes. Rinse.

Koji butter	(100%)	100 g butter
	(15%)	15 g Koji, dried (page 175)
Tokyo turnips and daikon		3–4 Tokyo turnips
		1 daikon
Plating	(100%)	50 g peas, shucked
		Pineappleweed greens, for garnish
		Lemon balm sprigs, for garnish
		Garden verbena, for garnish
		Pea flower, for garnish

Koji butter Bring butter to a simmer in a small saucepan. Remove from heat, then stir in koji. Set aside to steep for 10 minutes. Strain.

Tokyo turnips and daikon Using a mandoline, carefully slice turnips and daikon to a 2-mm (1⁄16-inch) thickness. (Make enough for 3 slices per person.) Cut out vegetables with a 2.5-cm (1-inch) round cookie cutter.

Plating Re-melt koji butter in a frying pan over medium heat. Add peas and prawn tail meat and heat until prawns are just cooked through.

Place peas in each bowl, then arrange prawns on top. Add dots of crème fraîche and finish with daikon, Tokyo turnips and garnishes.

In a saucepan, heat broth to a light simmer, then add to the bowl.

Vancouver Island Sea Salt

During a trip to Vancouver Island to visit Golden Eagle Black Cod, I was lucky enough to make a stop at Vancouver Island Sea Salt. We've been using their flake salt, including their smoked salt, at Perch since our opening. They're located twenty-six kilometres (sixteen miles) south of Campbell River on a giant property that backs onto the perfect spot to collect sea water.

When we arrived, we met up with the owner and co-founder, Scott Gibson, hopped into his Ford Bronco and toured the property. Making our way towards the ocean, we talked about the history of the business and property, his decision to sell salt and his future ideas. When Scott had returned to Canada after living abroad for over two decades, he and his wife noticed a huge lack in quality Canadian salts. Whereas other countries offer so many options of locally harvested sea salt, Canada didn't really have anything available—even though our country is bordered by three beautiful, clean oceans. So he researched the entire process of being in the salt business and discovered someone else who had also noticed the absence of Canadian sea salt. Scott reached out to him, they started chatting, and Scott got involved in the company at its infancy. In 2019, Scott bought out his partners and then continued to grow the company and took it from an extremely small (think tiny shed) operation to a very impressive set-up!

The physical location for the business was dictated by the ocean: Vancouver Island Sea Salt is situated where two different tides meet and create an incredibly clean and clear body of water. The water is cold, which is a big plus for seafood, so I assume the temperature is beneficial for the salt as well. The water is collected by a flexible pipe with a screen that helps to ensure that only water comes in (no rock, no seaweed and definitely no animals). No ecosystem interferes with this method of gathering the sea water. The water then travels through the small underground pipe (about 500 metres) to storage tanks. From there, it goes through multiple stages of filtration to remove any unwanted impurities. Then, it enters an ingenious piece of equipment that Scott created himself.

Because his unique method makes Vancouver Island Sea Salt the beautiful, high-quality product that it is, I won't go into too much detail about the equipment. Essentially, the "machine" raises the water salinity to an optimal percentage, then the water flows into large bins that look like maple syrup evaporator kettles (imagine giant metal vats about 30-cm/12-inches deep). As the water slowly heats up at a constant temperature, crystals form. The salt is harvested by hand from the top layer, then placed into an angled bin to drain out excess water. The salt is gently dehydrated and sorted again by hand according to strict quality control guidelines. From there, the salt is either packaged or sent to the company's smokehouse.

Their smoked salt is incredible. Once, one of our cooks opened a new container of smoked salt to put into our salt container. I was working on admin stuff at the bar and got a whiff of smoke. I leapt from my seat, searching everywhere to find out what was burning. It took me a solid ten minutes to realize that it was the freshly opened salt! The smoked salt is also one of my favourite ingredients for seasoning liquids. Not only does it add salinity to a broth or sauce, but it also introduces depth, smoke and umami. It's even become my not-so-secret ingredient when seasoning broths throughout service. (Our roasted garlic and vinegar broth needs to be adjusted several times during service because of its intensity—we want it right on the edge of "too aggressive.")

Vancouver Island Sea Salt does some cool things, but their vision of the future is looking especially awesome. For example, they reduce "smoke waste" by recapturing smoke from the process and reusing this by-product in other products. My immediate thought was to use the smoke as a fun addition for cocktails. The company also irrigates their land by reusing the freshwater that is a by-product of the salinity adjustment process.

Perch is committed to working with farmers and producers who share similar views with us about our impact on nature—and Vancouver Island Sea Salt's views are almost identical. We're so happy to have found their products and to be able to work closely with them. The future of this company is exciting, and what they're doing to keep the ocean and the wildlife around them unaffected by their products is truly commendable!

Scallop Macaron

Before Perch opened, someone reached out about contributing a recipe to a charity cookbook for Ottawa Therapy Dogs. (We were also asked to be part of a separate fundraiser for Shepherds of Good Hope.)

We created a tart filled with sturgeon mousse, gooseberry fluid gel, borage and violas, which became the foundation for this recipe; however, here we refined it with a silky smooth and delicate scallop mousse and a sweet yet savoury mustard macaron. It has since become a bit of a cult classic, with guests occasionally asking for seconds and talking about it for their whole meal.

Ground cherry fluid gel

Sunflower oil, for frying
(12.5%) 6 g shallot, sliced
(7.58%) 4 g garlic, sliced
(7.58%) 4 g ginger, sliced
(10%) 5 g Cointreau
(100%) 50 g pineapple ground cherries, husks removed
(50%) 25 g water
(10%) 5 g honey
(5%) 2.5 g apple cider vinegar
(1.5%) 0.75 g salt
(1%) 0.5 g citric acid
1.25% of total cooled weight agar-agar

Scallop mousse

Sunflower oil, for frying
(7%) 14 g shallot, sliced
(5%) 10 g garlic, sliced
Salt, to season
(100%) 200 g scallop
(3%) 6 g whisky
(25%) 50 g cubed butter, cold
(25%) 50 g whipping cream, cold

Macaron

(133%) 67 g almond flour
(222%) 111 g icing sugar
(100%) 50 g egg whites
(55.5%) 28 g sugar
(1%) 0.5 g salt
(7%) 3.5 g mustard powder

Plating

Smoked sea salt
Borage leaves
Viola petals

Ground cherry fluid gel Heat oil in a small saucepan over medium heat. Add shallot, garlic and ginger and sauté for 8 minutes, until translucent. Pour in Cointreau and cook for 1 minute (flambé if you like). Add the remaining ingredients except agar-agar and gently simmer for 30 minutes.

Transfer the mixture to a high-powered blender and purée. Pour into a container, then refrigerate until cooled.

Combine the mixture and agar-agar in a saucepan and bring to a simmer, whisking continuously. Pour into a container and refrigerate overnight until firm.

Roughly cut the firm gel with a knife and place back in the blender. Blend on high speed until smooth. Pass through a fine-mesh strainer, then place in a squeeze bottle.

Scallop mousse Note: For the mousse to blend properly, we make more than needed.

Heat oil in a frying pan over medium heat. Add shallot, garlic and salt and sauté for 8 minutes, until translucent. Do not caramelize. Add scallop and gently cook for a few minutes but do not allow the mixture to colour. Pour in whisky and flambé.

Once whisky is burned off, stir in butter and cream and gently warm until butter has completely melted, reaching no more than a very gentle simmer. Remove from heat and cool to 45°C (113°F).

Pour mousse into a high-powered blender and blend until smooth. Pass through a fine-mesh strainer into a container. Refrigerate until cold.

Transfer mousse to a piping bag with the #124 petal tip.

Macaron Sift almond flour and icing sugar together into a bowl.

In an Ankarsrum, whip egg whites until foamy and opaque. (Alternatively, use a stand mixer fitted with the appropriate attachment.) Gradually add in sugar and whip to stiff peaks. Add meringue and the remaining ingredients to the bowl with the flour mixture and macaronage.

Transfer the mixture to a piping bag and pipe to the desired size, tapping your tray to pop any air bubbles. Set aside to dry for 20–40 minutes, until a nice film forms.

Preheat a Unox combi oven to 148°C (300°F).

Bake for 18 minutes at fan level 1 and 10% extraction. Makes about 15.

Plating Pipe scallop mousse onto macarons in a steady back and forth motion. Season with a little smoked sea salt. Place 5 dots of ground cherry fluid gel on top. Garnish with borage leaves and viola petals.

Scallop and Sunchoke

If I could have only a single bite of one ingredient, without any sauce or components to it (minus butter for basting, of course), I would choose a scallop from the coldest waters possible. Scallop has everything—texture, sweetness, umami—rendering it a perfect bite of food (for me, at least). Sunchoke and celeriac add more sweetness as well as earthiness. The caviar just gives this dish a beautiful salinity with more umami depth!

Sunchoke foam

Sunflower oil, for frying
(40%) 120 g shallot, sliced
(5%) 15 g garlic, sliced
(3%) 9 g ginger, sliced
(100%) 300 g sunchoke, sliced
(20%) 60 g shiitake mushroom, sliced
(3%) 9 g Dijon mustard
(0.7%) 2 g dulse
(100%) 300 g Seaweed Water (page 175)
(60%) 180 g oat milk
(4%) 12 g balsamic vinegar
(2.5%) 7.5 g shoyu
(2.5%) 7.5 g birch syrup

Brown butter celeriac

1 medium-large celeriac
(100%) 50 g brown butter
(10%) 5 g birch syrup

Plating

6 U-10 scallops
Flake sea salt, to season
(100%) 90 g celery, peeled and finely diced
Neutral oil, for frying
Butter, for basting
Alder catkins, in a pepper mill, to season
Hazelnuts, shelled, for sprinkling
(26.7%) 24 g caviar
Cornflower petals, for garnish

Sunchoke foam Heat oil in a saucepan over medium heat. Add shallot, garlic and ginger and sauté for 10 minutes, until translucent. Add sunchoke and shiitake and sauté for another 10 minutes, until soft. Add Dijon and dulse.

Pour in seaweed water and simmer until reduced by half. Stir in oat milk and cook for another 10 minutes. Remove from heat, then add vinegar, shoyu and birch syrup.

Transfer to a high-powered blender and blitz until smooth. Pass through a fine-mesh strainer. Keep warm.

Brown butter celeriac Using the smallest melon baller, melon ball celeriac.

Add brown butter to a frying pan over medium heat. Stir in birch syrup, whisking to emulsify. Add celeriac and cook for 4–5 minutes, until just tender. Drain, then set aside.

Plating Clean scallops, removing the abductor muscle and reserving it for XO sauce (page 84) or garum (page 178). Season with flake sea salt and set aside for 5–10 minutes.

Pour sunchoke foam into an insulated siphon and charge with one N2O charger.

Place 15 brown butter celeriac balls into each bowl, then sprinkle celery on top.

Heat enough oil to coat the bottom of a frying pan over medium heat. Place the drier side of each scallop into the pan and pan-fry for 5 minutes, until golden. Flip scallops, then add a knob of butter and baste. Cook until scallops are just cooked but almost raw in the centre. Transfer scallops to a tray. Season with flake sea salt and alder catkins.

Add enough sunchoke foam to each bowl to cover the base by 2 cm (¾ inch). Add scallops, golden side up. Using a microplane, grate hazelnuts on top. Finish with a quenelle of caviar. Garnish with cornflower petals.

Smoked Sturgeon and Carrot

Everything for this course fell into place on the first try. With an excess of brined, hot-smoked sturgeon loins to work through, I thinly sliced them, laid them out on a silicone sheet and froze them. Once frozen, they were perfectly cut into beautiful discs, and the leftover sturgeon trimming was combined with mushroom and squash (from two other dishes) to create an XO-style condiment. Then, I had a large Cambro of beautiful carrots from a local farm to make the caramelized carrot sauce. It all just came together like a well-built puzzle as I conceptualized the dish, and I achieved the intended result on the first try—which rarely happens.

Buddha's hand syrup

(100%) 75 g water
(85%) 64 g sugar
Peel of 1 O'Citrus Buddha's hand citrus

Sturgeon disc

(100%) 1 kg water
(5%) 50 g salt
(5%) 50 g sake
(2.5%) 25 g maple syrup
(0.5%) 5 g garlic, sliced
(0.2%) 2 g sweet paprika
(100%) 1 kg sturgeon loin

Caramelized carrots

(100%) 500 g carrot
(1.5%) 8 g salt
(0.5%) 2.5 g baking soda
(16%) 80 g butter, melted

Caramelized carrot and sake sauce

(100%) 200 g Caramelized Carrots (see here)
(46%) 92 g carrot juice
(34%) 68 g sake
(33%) 66 g filtered water
(23%) 46 g verjus
(19%) 38 g honey
(14%) 28 g mirin
(12%) 24 g Lacto-Koji Water (page 176)
(3%) 6 g salt

Squash XO

(100%) 250 g sunflower oil (divided)
(10%) 25 g garlic, microplaned
(9%) 23 g ginger, brunoise
(88%) 220 g sturgeon, brunoise
(35%) 88 g mushroom, such as shiitake, brunoise
(3%) 8 g salt
(133%) 333 g squash pulp (reserved from juicing)
(25%) 63 g miso
(14%) 35 g gochujang
(100%) 250 g fresh squash juice

Buddha's hand syrup Combine water and sugar in a saucepan and bring to a simmer. Add citrus peel.

Refrigerate for 5 days to infuse. Strain.

Sturgeon disc Combine all ingredients except sturgeon in a saucepan and bring to a simmer. Set aside to cool, then refrigerate until cooled completely.

Place sturgeon in marinade and refrigerate for 48 hours.

In a smoker set to 100°C (212°F), hot-smoke sturgeon until it reaches an internal temperature of 65°C (149°F).

Using a meat slicer, slice sturgeon into 1.5-mm (1⁄24-inch) thick slices. On a Silpat®, overlap each slice onto a third of the previous slice. Freeze until hard. (This makes it easier to cut them properly into discs.)

Using an 8-cm (3¼-inch) ring mould, cut sturgeon slices into discs. Keep them separated between layers of parchment paper until needed. Reserve the leftover sturgeon trim for the final assembly.

Caramelized carrots Note: To achieve the correct pressure, we make more than needed.

Place all ingredients in a pressure cooker with the butter added last. Do not toss or cool down the butter. Cook on high for 50 minutes. Force release.

Caramelized carrot and sake sauce Combine all ingredients in a high-powered blender and blitz until smooth. Pass through a fine-mesh strainer.

Squash XO Heat a small amount of oil in a saucepan over medium heat. Add garlic and ginger and sauté for 8 minutes. Add sturgeon, mushroom and salt and cook for another 6 minutes. Stir in squash pulp, miso and gochujang. Reduce heat to low and cook for 5 minutes.

Pour in squash juice and simmer for 5 minutes. Add the remaining oil and hold on low heat for 15 minutes, stirring every 3 minutes to prevent the bottom from burning. Set aside to cool.

Bok choy and squash XO

(8%) 32 g butter
(50%) 200 g Squash XO (see here), plus extra if needed
(100%) 400 g bok choy, chiffonade
(0.5%) 2 g salt, plus extra to taste

Toasted millet

(100%) 100 g millet, toasted
Camelina oil, for tossing
Salt, to taste

Roasted carrots

(100%) 300 g carrot, cut into bite-size pieces
(2.3%) 7 g salt
Camelina oil, to coat

Watermelon radish

1 watermelon radish, sliced with a mandoline

Plating

(100%) 125 g reserved sturgeon trim from Sturgeon Disc (see here), diced

Bok choy and squash XO Melt butter in a frying pan over medium heat. Add squash XO, bok choy and salt and cook for 5 minutes. Season with more squash XO and salt.

Toasted millet Bring a small saucepan of water to a boil. Add millet and boil for 8 minutes, until al dente. Drain, then set aside to cool. Toss with oil and season with salt.

Roasted carrots Preheat oven to 220°C (425°F).

Combine all ingredients in a bowl and toss. Transfer to a baking sheet and roast for 8 minutes, until cooked through with a slight bite.

Watermelon radish Using a 3.5-cm (1½-inch) ring mould, cut out discs. Cut each disc in half.

Plating Place the 8-cm (3¼-inch) ring mould in the centre of each bowl. Press toasted millet into the mould, about 3-mm (⅛-inch) deep. Sprinkle 20 g of sturgeon dice on top. Randomly place 5 carrot pieces into millet. Top with bok choy and squash XO, pressing the mixture to a depth of 1 cm (½ inch). Lightly coat with Buddha's hand syrup.

Carefully remove the ring mould. Place a frozen sturgeon disc on top. On a slight angle, overlap watermelon radish around the mound. Pour sauce around sturgeon disc.

 Smoked Sturgeon and Carrot, p.128

Acadian Sturgeon and Caviar

I met Cornel and Dorina Ceapa of Acadian Sturgeon and Caviar in 2014. Cornel's knowledge of sturgeon is second to none, and he has taught me an incredible amount about the subject, from eggs to environmentally sound fishing practices to high-quality farming designed to mimic nature; it was so inspiring and energizing to talk with someone so passionate about a specific topic. He supports both wild and farmed methods with the belief that the combined practice is the most sustainable avenue. The company's wild sturgeon program involves Atlantic sturgeon, a species that can grow up to 380 cm (150 inches) in length, whereas their farmed program focuses on the shortnose sturgeon, which are much smaller at 137 cm (54 inches) and raised in extremely large tanks, on land, using recirculated water from the St. John River. Cornel's mission is to raise his fish stock at the level of Mother Nature (in other words, as naturally as possible without compromising Mother Nature). The company also farms Atlantic sturgeon, but the oldest fish they have raised at this point are seven years old now; Atlantic sturgeon need to be twelve years old before they start maturing and producing caviar.

I had promoted and sold Acadian Sturgeon and Caviar for nearly a decade before I made the trip to New Brunswick to see what they do first-hand. We woke at 4 AM and hit the road. The drive to the hatchery is just under an hour from Saint John, and you get there by crossing a river by ferry. (Interestingly, the ferry operates with an underwater pulley system that tugs the ferry from one side to the other.) It was nearly 6 AM by the time we boarded the ferry, and we made our way to the first net to meet up with the two fishermen. The fog rolling across the water was so dense, we couldn't see anything beyond six metres (twenty feet); in fact, we had to navigate with a GPS system to find the nets.

Net-fishing gets a lot of flak, and I understand why and normally agree. However, when fishing for large sturgeons in waters with smaller fish, fishermen can use larger fishing nets with 35-cm (14-inch) openings and have next to no bycatch whatsoever. Any bycatch tends to be shortnose sturgeons. Sturgeon is a uniquely calm fish species, so the net doesn't bother them much. When they swim into the net, the holes are large enough for the smaller fish to swim through, while the ones that get caught are done so without their gills getting snagged in the nets and they can still breathe without any problems. If a fish were to die in the net, or if the net caused too much stress, it would damage the eggs and/or meat (which is bad for business), so everything is done to minimize harm and ensure that the sturgeons are calm and able to breathe.

Acadian Sturgeon and Caviar have two fishermen, who are DFO licensed and have a total of eleven nets on the St. John River, each one fifty metres (fifty-four yards) wide. Net placement is very important.

(The area of the river where they fish is roughly 2000 metres/2187 yards.) On the day we went out, the first net was the most fruitful, with four fish, only one of which was female. The company follows an annual quota of 175 males and 175 females, and they apply a size restriction even more rigorous than government regulations to ensure that their fishing practices help with wild population growth. A few fish were caught in two more nets, but another two were completely skunked. It didn't matter: the incredible scenery with the fog dissipating at the break of dawn made it all worthwhile. This was my first time in the Maritimes, and the scenery did not disappoint—it was beautiful!

By 8 AM, we had arrived at the final net, which had caught a couple of fish, with one being the biggest catch of the day. Overall, eleven fish were caught, but only eight were kept. Smaller fish, as well as females with substandard egg quality (confirmed via a quick egg biopsy), are released. Every fish is also tagged so in-depth stats (journey, age, growth, etc.) can be tracked. For instance, one of the fish that Cornel kept this year was caught and tracked eight years ago when it was much smaller, and he had an in-depth log for it.

Acadian Sturgeon and Caviar's incredible farmed program uses water from the St. John River to raise the fish. With the program's powerful filtration process, cleaner water returns to the river. At their fish farm in Carters Point, they have male and female breeding stocks as well as a hatchery where they raise the sturgeon from egg to one year old. They have another location a few hours away with thirty-two giant 20,000-gallon tanks, where they raise their sturgeon from this point on. Unfortunately, I didn't make it to this location to see the process, but I imagine it is completely dialled in.

I completely lucked out because the farmed females were starting the spawning process due to the water temperatures being just right! We also harvested sperm from the males and ovulated eggs from the females by C-section. Each batch of fertilized eggs was placed in individual incubation chambers. It takes a decade for an egg to mature to an adult female with roe for caviar production.

When wild Atlantic sturgeon is caught, it is fully broken down and ready to ship within a few hours. In that same amount of time, the caviar is also cleaned using just salt as a preservative (a lot of caviar companies will often use Borax) and cured in a room that is UV sterilized daily. This ensures that everything is as clean as possible, and the caviar has no chance of contamination.

Acadian Sturgeon and Caviar is committed to the animals, the ecosystem and the final product. Cornel has spent his life's work creating a sustainable process for breeding and farming top-quality sturgeon. The process blew my mind, and I will always remember being a part of that experience. It feels awesome knowing that the farmed caviar I buy a decade from now could be from the eggs that I helped to fertilize and incubate. (Okay, I didn't help all that much, but I was there to hold a few tails.)

After the fishing trip and the facility tour, Cornel prepared magnums of Champagne, sparkling Canadian wine, sake and food to showcase the (wild and farmed) fish and caviar. Cornel and Dorina's hospitality and our experience with them were simply amazing. I'm proud to use their products and to call them friends.

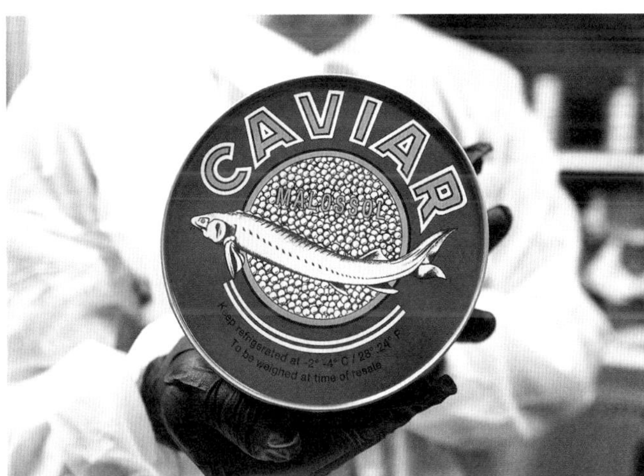

CAVIAR
MALOSSOL
Keep refrigerated at -2°-4° C / 28°-24° F
To be weighed at time of resale

Unagi Black Cod Chawanmushi

In my opinion, no fish in our waters showcases the quality of our seafood better than black cod, and this is especially true of fish from Kyuquot-Checleset, British Columbia! This versatile fish can hold up to any form of cooking, from raw to grilled over charcoal. It's beautiful and always tastes great.

In this dish, the sweet, buttery fish is complemented with a deep umami marinade and a hard smokiness thanks to a char from the grill. I often crave black cod done in this exact way.

We also barrel-aged the sake to give it greater depth of flavour, but this is entirely optional.

Sea truffle base

- (100%) 220 g water
- (7%) 16 g Koji, dried (page 175)
- (0.9%) 2 g dulse
- (0.7%) 1.5 g bull kelp
- (0.5%) 1 g sea truffle

Unagi black cod

- (100%) 250 g mirin
- (100%) 250 g shoyu
- (10%) 25 g sake
- (5%) 13 g honey
- (5%) 13 g sugar
- (5%) 13 g verjus
- 1 black cod, cleaned

Sea truffle dashi

- (100%) 100 g Sea Truffle Base (see here)
- (8%) 8 g mirin
- (5%) 5 g shoyu

Charred cucumber sauce

- (100%) 125 g cucumber
- (70%) 88 g poultry stock
- (13.5%) 17 g reserved unagi sauce from Unagi Black Cod, (see here)
- (1.5%) 1.9 g salt

Sea truffle custard base

- (100%) 100 g Sea Truffle Dashi (see here)
- (75%) 75 g eggs

Plating

- 5 shiitake mushrooms, medium dice
- Smoked sea salt, to season
- 1 cucumber, peeled and brunoise
- 1 carrot, julienned and soaked in ice water until curled, for garnish
- Micro Thai basil or the smallest leaves, for garnish
- Cornflower petals, for garnish

Sea truffle base Combine all ingredients in a container and mix well. Refrigerate for 48 hours.

Strain, reserving seaweed for another use. (It can be re-steeped.)

Unagi black cod Mix all ingredients except black cod in a saucepan and gently simmer, until reduced to a third of the original amount. Set aside to cool.

Cut black cod into 50-g portions. Combine black cod and unagi sauce and refrigerate overnight to marinate.

Skewer black cod with BBQ-safe metal skewers. Reserve unagi sauce for charred cucumber sauce and plating.

Sea truffle dashi Combine all ingredients in a bowl and mix well.

Charred cucumber sauce Preheat a grill.

Add cucumber and char on all sides. Don't be afraid to burn it a bit. Place in a hotel pan with a lid. Refrigerate until cooled.

Combine all ingredients in a high-powered blender and blend until smooth.

Sea truffle custard base Combine all ingredients in a bowl and mix well.

Plating Preheat a combi oven to 99°C (210°F). Also, preheat a Konro grill.

Combine 50 g of custard base and 10 g of shiitake each in 6 heatproof bowls. Steam in a combi oven on the top rack for 5½ minutes with full steam, until set with some wiggle to it. Season with smoked sea salt.

Meanwhile, place black cod on the grill. Grill for 5–10 minutes, glazing with the remaining unagi sauce, until black cod starts to flake slightly. Remove from heat, then remove the skin. It should come off easily.

Place 15 g of cucumber on top of the chawanmushi. Spoon over enough cucumber sauce to cover by 2–3 mm (1/16–1/8 inch). Place black cod on top, then garnish with a small pile of carrot, 3 Thai basil leaves and cornflower petals.

Golden Eagle Black Cod

Canada has incredible seafood—arguably, the best in the world. (Okay, I'm slightly biased.) And it's not only our seafood that is amazing but also our freshwater fish (shout-out to Affinity Fish and their high-quality freshwater fish from the Great Lakes). A chef once told me that Canada exports its best seafood to other countries willing to spend top dollar for our products, leaving us with third- or fourth-tier Canadian seafood.

Our country is surrounded by cold water, which is great for fish and shellfish because photosynthesis occurs at a quicker rate in the cold and thus elevates the oxygen in the water. The result? A healthier and cleaner environment for the animals. Cold water also slows down the growth rate of the animals and prevents salt water from permeating the flesh of the animals, resulting in firmer and sweeter meat. Black cod, also known as sablefish, is a prime example!

Golden Eagle Black Cod knows this, and they know fish! Terry Brooks, the managing director, is an early pioneer in the production of black cod culture. He comes from a family of multi-generational fishermen, farmers and mongers, and he has worked with fish, one way or another, his entire life—and, to no surprise, his knowledge is truly remarkable.

But he decided to do things a little differently when he started his own farm: he focused on black cod. While salmon farming can be sustainable (for example, in New Zealand), it hasn't had the best reputation, and salmon are not ideal to farm, based on their life cycles and habits alone.

Terry looked at black cod because they're slow-moving fish that can often be found "relaxing" near the bottom of the ocean in a single spot. They also enjoy very deep waters, thus requiring less oxygen in the water than other fish species such as salmon. In fact, black cod can thrive in a farmed environment.

To start the company, he began working with biologists to better understand the reproductive process in black cod and thus optimize their farming. A hatchery was built on Salt Spring Island in British Columbia where the company has a team of experts who dedicate their lives to taking care of the brood stock as well as raising black cod from eggs. Gigantic tanks are filled with brood stock (females in one, males in another), and when the females are ready to breed, the eggs are mixed with cryogenically frozen milt. This keeps the genetic pool very large and the stock healthy.

The eggs hatch in forty days in a pitch-black room in blackout tanks to prevent any light from entering, which can harm the life of the fish—hence their preference in the wild to fertilize their eggs in the very deep ocean. Once the fish hatch and consume the entire yolk sac, they are fed live zooplankton that are grown in a room next to the nursery. Golden Eagle Black Cod grows their own zooplankton for their fish, to ensure that they have a constant high-grade supply for their hatchlings.

Once the fish outgrow the hatchery, they are transported to a grow-out farm in Kyuquot Sound where they swim in giant netted pens (over 27 million litres and up to 35 metres deep). The water here is pristine and well flushed. When we dropped the ROV into the pens to get a look at the fish, it was a challenge to locate them because the pens are vast and they have so much space to swim around. The fish feed on high-grade fish food while a team member observes them with an underwater camera. As soon as the fish appear to be full and a pellet or two passes them, the feeding is stopped. This helps to reduce waste and minimizes the impact on the ecosystem by mitigating negative side effects that would occur if wild stock were to eat the food (which would not harm the fish in any way). And as fish food is the greatest expense in raising fish, this process ensures that no money is wasted.

The fish live here until they are two and a half years old. After they've been ethically harvested at this age, they are placed in a deep chill ice slush to preserve the quality of the fish.

Golden Eagle Black Cod does an incredible job at working with nature to raise a delicious and very nutritious product for consumption. They have some of the best fish you can get anywhere and are an operation led by quality, ethical production and sustainability for the planet! They also work in partnership with Kyuquot-Checleset (Ka:'yu:'k't'h'/Che:k:tles7et'h') First Nations.

Chef Jade Berg was our guide on this trip, and he has become a great friend. He organized the entirety of the trip and set up a top-notch itinerary, including a tour of Vancouver Island Sea Salt (page 120), an overnight fishing excursion on the open ocean, prawn trapping (put this on your bucket list if you've never had fresh-out-of-the-water, raw prawns) and oyster harvesting. We even walked around an early nineteenth-century whaling station. It was my first time catching a salmon and seeing the semi-aquatic Vancouver Coastal Sea wolf. This trip was an unforgettable experience for me and my photographer, Sarah Farmer, and we're so grateful for Terry, Chef Berg and the Golden Eagle Black Cod team.

desserts

Chaga Cake and Black Garlic Ice Cream, p.144

Chaga Cake and Black Garlic Ice Cream

This dessert has been the second-most controversial dish at Perch. (See page 44 for our most divisive.) Everything works perfectly together from a flavour profile perspective, and visually, it's fun and simple. But as soon as garlic is mentioned in a dessert, people dismiss it immediately and, occasionally, get angry—not realizing that black garlic has immense sweetness.

Once we changed the name from Black Garlic Ice Cream to Sake Ice Cream, perceptions changed and there was no more pushback. This dessert also ties in birch trees with the chaga mushrooms that grow on them.

Dehydrated birch meringue

- (100%) 75 g egg whites
- (6%) 4.5 g verjus
- (200%) 150 g sugar
- (90%) 68 g birch syrup
- Non-stick cooking spray

Black garlic ice cream

- (100%) 30 g black garlic
- (533%) 160 g milk
- (170%) 51 g sugar
- (126%) 37.8 g egg yolks
- (4.5%) 1.4 g salt
- (100%) 30 g sake
- (333%) 100 g whipping cream

Chaga cake

- Non-stick cooking spray
- (100%) 360 g sugar
- (100%) 360 g all-purpose flour
- (3.6%) 13 g baking soda
- (1.5%) 5 g salt
- (15%) 54 g dried chaga powder
- (55%) 198 g sunflower oil
- (166%) 598 g milk
- (10%) 36 g white vinegar

Dehydrated birch meringue In an Ankarsrum, whip egg whites and verjus to soft peaks. (Alternatively, use a stand mixer fitted with the appropriate attachment.)

Meanwhile, combine sugar and just enough water to dissolve the sugar in a saucepan over medium-high heat. Boil until the temperature reaches 115°C (240°F).

Slowly pour sugar water into meringue while whisking continuously. Let cool on medium speed. Pour in birch syrup, scraping the sides of the bowl until well incorporated.

Spray a sheet of acetate with non-stick cooking spray. Spread meringue thinly over top. Place in a dehydrator set at 50°C (122°F) for 2 hours.

Using a 7-cm (2¾-inch) ring mould, cut into discs. Cut each disc in half. Finish dehydrating for 5 hours, until fully crispy.

Black garlic ice cream In a high-powered blender, combine black garlic and milk and blend.

In a Thermomix fitted with the whisk attachment, combine sugar, egg yolks and salt. Mix at speed 3 until well combined. Add sake. Set the heat to 80°C (175°F) and timer to 20 minutes. Wait 4 minutes.

Add the milk–black garlic mixture and cream and swirl to mix well, grabbing any bits of black garlic that were left behind. Once the temperature reaches 80°C (175°F), set timer to 10 minutes.

When the time is up, place the mixture in a thin layer in a hotel pan with plastic wrap touching the mixture and refrigerate to chill. Once cold, churn in an ice-cream machine.

Chaga cake Preheat a combi oven to 150°C (300°F) with 50% fan. Line a half sheet pan with a Silpat® and spray with non-stick cooking spray.

Sift dry ingredients into a bowl.

Combine oil and milk in another bowl, then whisk with dry ingredients. Stir in vinegar until just mixed, then transfer the mixture to the prepared pan. Bake for 35 minutes. Set aside to cool, then refrigerate to cool completely.

Using a 7-cm (2¾-inch) ring mould, cut out rounds. Cut each round in half so they're semi-circles.

Haskap fluid gel

(100%) 200 g haskaps
(50%) 100 g water
(25%) 50 g sugar
1.25% of total cooled weight agar-agar

Nocino anglaise

(170%) 85 g egg yolks
(120%) 60 g sugar
(100%) 50 g nocino (walnut liqueur)
(320%) 160 g whipping cream

Haskap fluid gel In a saucepan, combine haskaps, water and sugar and simmer for 10 minutes, until haskaps are fully cooked.

Transfer to a blender and blitz until smooth. Set aside to cool to room temperature.

Pour the mixture into a separate saucepan, add 1.25% (of total weight) agar-agar and bring to a simmer while whisking. Transfer to a container and refrigerate until completely set.

Blitz in a high-powered blender on high speed until smooth. Pass through a fine-mesh strainer.

Nocino anglaise Place egg yolks and sugar in a Thermomix fitted with the whisk attachment. Mix at speed 2.5 until well emulsified. Slowly pour in nocino. Set the temperature to 80°C (175°F) and the time to 12 minutes.

When the time is up, slowly pour in cream. Strain liquid into a heatproof container. Place a piece of plastic wrap on the surface and refrigerate until cooled.

Plating Add a line of haskap fluid gel to one side of each bowl. Pour enough nocino anglaise to cover the base. Add a chaga cake, covering half of the gel. Place a quenelle of ice cream next to cake. Place a dehydrated meringue semi-circle on top.

Chestnut Cake and Parsnip Ice Cream

I'm not really a sweets person (unless the sweet is a gummy candy), and I will work with chocolate only if I have to. I've spent most of my career in the savoury part of restaurants, and I lean towards sweeter vegetables for my desserts.

Parsnips are very underrated, but they are delicious—especially after a frost or two, which adds sweetness to the root veg. Our good friend Tu Le, who happens to be one of the most talented pastry chefs I've ever met, joined the team when Perch opened. Instructing him not to use chocolate but vegetables in a dessert may have been a shock to his system, but this dessert was the perfect ending to our opening tasting menu.

Caramelized parsnips	(100%)	500 g parsnip
	(16%)	80 g butter, melted
	(1.5%)	8 g salt
	(0.5%)	2.5 g baking soda
Caramelized parsnip ice cream	(100%)	150 g hot Caramelized Parsnips (see here)
	(500%)	750 g milk
	(166%)	249 g whipping cream
	(100%)	150 g egg yolks
	(87%)	130 g sugar
Chestnut cake	(100%)	288 g eggs
	(72.9%)	210 g sugar
	(67.7%)	195 g chestnut flour
	(2.1%)	6 g baking powder
	(1.5%)	4.3 g salt
	(88.5%)	255 g butter, melted
Maple and verjus reduction	(100%)	100 g maple syrup
	(100%)	100 g verjus
Crispy parsnip		1 parsnip
		Birch syrup, to coat

Caramelized parsnips Note: To achieve the correct pressure, we make more than needed.

Combine all ingredients in a pressure cooker. Cook on high for 50 minutes. Force release.

Caramelized parsnip ice cream In a high-powered blender, combine caramelized parsnips, milk and cream and blitz until smooth.

Combine egg yolks and sugar in a Thermomix fitted with the whisk attachment. Mix at speed 2.5 until well incorporated. Set the temperature to 80°C (175°F) and timer to 30 minutes and slowly pour in the parsnip and dairy mixture. Once the mixture reaches the above temperature, set the timer to 10 minutes.

When the time is up, pour through a fine-mesh strainer, then refrigerate to cool.

Transfer the mixture to an ice-cream machine and churn.

Chestnut cake Preheat oven to 175°C (347°F). Line a half sheet tray with a Silpat®.

Whisk eggs for 8 minutes in an Ankarsrum. (Alternatively, use a stand mixer fitted with the appropriate attachment.) Slowly add sugar. Fold in chestnut flour, baking powder and salt. Fold in butter. Spread on the tray. Bake for 16 minutes, until golden.

Using a 6-cm (2½-inch) round cookie cutter, cut out circles.

Maple and verjus reduction Combine both ingredients and cook in a saucepan over medium-high heat until the mixture reaches 112°C (233°F).

Crispy parsnip Preheat oven to 175°C (347°F). Place a Silpat® on a tray.

Peel ribbons of parsnip. Place in a bowl, then lightly coat in birch syrup. Transfer to the prepared tray. Bake for 8 minutes, until golden and dried.

Plating Place 1 cake on each serving plate or bowl. Top with a quenelle of ice cream. Drizzle with reduction. Garnish with crispy parsnip.

Rhubarb and Elderflower

Chef Tu Le's precision and passion came together in this perfect expression of Perch. Ottawan chefs look forward most to the first rhubarb harvest of the year because it heralds warmer weather and new produce to come. We work mainly with Bower Farm (page 51) for the rhubarb, and they also grow ginger, which makes an ideal complement to fresh or cooked rhubarb.

Toasted alder adds a citrusy, peppery note, taking this sorbet over the edge with a unique and delicious flavour profile. Plus, we never tire of our guests' reaction when they see us making bubbles for dessert!

You'll need an aquarium pump to aerate the elderflower syrup.

Duck fat crumble

(100%) 260 g all-purpose flour
(42.3%) 110 g icing sugar
(42.3%) 110 g salt
(42.3%) 110 g chilled duck fat
1 egg

Rhubarb sorbet

(100%) 300 g rhubarb, red pieces, chopped
(25%) 75 g sugar
(6%) 18 g liquid glucose

Ginger fluid gel

(100%) 175 g water
(100%) 175 g sugar
(25%) 44 g grated ginger
(12%) 21 g sake
(1% of above total weight)
~4 g agar-agar

Poached rhubarb

(100%) 200 g sugar
(100%) 200 g water
18 stalks rhubarb, cut into diamonds

Duck fat crumble In a food processor, combine flour, icing sugar and salt. Add duck fat and pulse until the texture is sandy. Add egg and pulse until just combined.

Knead the dough by hand until it comes together. Rest for 1 hour.

Preheat a combi oven to 180°C (350°F) with 50% fan.

Roll out the dough to a 2–3-mm (1⁄16–1⁄8-inch) thickness. Bake for 10 minutes, until golden brown.

Once cooled, break up the dough in the food processor till a crumble is achieved.

Rhubarb sorbet Combine all ingredients in a saucepan and set aside to macerate for 30 minutes. Gently simmer for 20 minutes, until rhubarb has softened.

Transfer to a high-powered blender and blitz until smooth. Strain.

Transfer to an ice-cream machine and churn.

Ginger fluid gel Combine all ingredients in a saucepan and bring to a simmer. Refrigerate until cooled and set.

Transfer to a high-powered blender and blitz. Strain through a fine-mesh strainer.

Poached rhubarb Combine sugar and water in a saucepan and bring to a simmer. Add rhubarb, then remove from heat. Set aside to cool.

Elderflower bubbles

(100%) 200 g water
(30%) 60 g elderflower cordial
(0.65%) 1.3 g Versawhip
(0.33%) 0.66 g xanthan gum

Toasted alder

(100%) 20 g alder catkin

Plating

Anise hyssop, for garnish

Elderflower bubbles Combine all ingredients in a high-powered blender and mix. Strain.

Toasted alder Toast alder in a frying pan over medium heat, until aromatic. Transfer to a pepper grinder.

Plating Place a spoonful of duck fat crumble on each plate. Add 3 poached rhubarb pieces next to it. Squeeze 7 dots of ginger fluid gel on poached rhubarb and around crumble. Place a quenelle of sorbet over crumble. Mill a small amount of alder catkin on sorbet and garnish with anise hyssop.

Using an aquarium pump, aerate elderflower syrup and make large bubbles. (You can have the pump going before you start to plate; just keep an eye on the bubbles so they don't overflow in the container.) Using a large spoon, scoop out bubbles and place them over the dessert.

Rhubarb and Elderflower, p.148

Squash and Sourdough, p.152

Squash and Sourdough

Often, I'll text our staff group chat, "Is this cool or dumb?" For this creation, I had asked them if it was cool or dumb for our first and our last (dessert) course to use the same ingredients, with one being savoury and the other being sweet. The consensus was that it was a super cool idea, and it turned out that the guests thought "bookending" the tasting menu was fun. It was also a great way to use up the "scraps" from cutting out perfectly rectangular pieces of squash from the first dish (page 54).

Squash purée

(100%) 300 g roasted squash
(42%) 126 g water

Squash tuile

(100%) 125 g Squash Purée (see here)
(27%) 34 g icing sugar
(33%) 41 g isomalt powder
(6%) 8 g glucose

Squash "compote"

(100%) 150 g squash, brunoise
(30%) 45 g sugar
(60%) 90 g water
(40%) 60 g Squash Purée (see here)

Sourdough ice cream

(100%) 250 g milk
(100%) 250 g whipping cream
(77%) 193 g sourdough bread
(20%) 50 g egg yolks
(16%) 40 g sugar
Sourdough bread discard equivalent to 10% of weight of dairy once strained

Squash purée Blend both ingredients until smooth. Strain through a bouillon strainer.

Squash tuile Preheat oven to 105°C (221°F).

Combine all ingredients in a high-powered blender and blend. Strain through a bouillon strainer.

Using a rectangle stencil, spread the mixture over a Silpat®, making 6 rectangles. Bake for 35 minutes. Carefully peel rectangles off while still hot and wrap each around separate cylinder moulds 1 cm (½ inch) in diameter. Set aside to cool.

Once cooled, slide tuile off the mould.

Squash "compote" Combine all ingredients except squash purée in a saucepan and cook over medium heat, until just tender. Strain, then cool. Fold in squash purée.

Sourdough ice cream Combine milk and cream in a bowl. Add bread and soak overnight.

Strain out as much liquid in the bread mixture as possible. Measure the weight of the liquid.

Combine egg yolks and sugar in a Thermomix fitted with the whisk attachment.

Mix at speed 2.5 until well incorporated. Set the temperature to 80°C (175°F) and timer to 30 minutes and slowly pour in the strained dairy and the sourdough discard. Once the mixture reaches the above temperature, set the timer to 10 minutes.

When the time is up, pour through a fine-mesh strainer, then refrigerate to cool.

Transfer the mixture to an ice-cream machine and churn.

Burnt apple purée

(100%) 250 g Granny Smith apples, cored and quartered

Buckwheat granola

(100%) 200 g buckwheat
(38%) 76 g maple syrup

Plating

Cornflower petals, for garnish

Burnt apple purée Preheat oven to 150°C (300°F).

Place apples on a baking mat and bake for 20 minutes, until browned and completely softened.

In a blender, blend until smooth. Pass through a fine-mesh strainer.

Buckwheat granola Preheat oven to 150°C (300°F). Line a sheet tray with a Silpat®.

Combine both ingredients in a bowl and toss together. Place the mixture on the prepared sheet tray. Bake for 8 minutes. Set aside to cool.

For a finer granola, transfer to a high-powered blender and pulse.

Plating Place a line of apple purée on each plate, about the length of squash tuile. Fill a pastry bag with squash compote and carefully fill squash tuile. Place tuile next to apple purée. Add a spoonful of buckwheat granola next to it. Place a scoop of ice cream on the granola. Garnish with a few cornflower petals.

cocktails

O'Citrus

When we opened the restaurant, we decided not to use citrus in the kitchen or in the bar program. It's a very wasteful ingredient that usually ends up, one way or another, in the garbage. However, when we can get the Canadian citrus out of Quebec, we bring it in. It's seldom available, and there's not a lot of it when it is.

In Laval, Quebec, Vyckie Vaillancourt started a small passion project greenhouse farm on her large conventional farm, O'Citrus. During our visit, we walked past tons of onions curing on rows of tables, squash and other produce and reached a small greenhouse tucked behind much larger ones used to create cool living statues that are shipped across North America.

After her family brought over a citrus tree from Japan, it became a small obsession for Vyckie. The greenhouse is now filled with beautiful Japanese citrus trees, all in their own buckets, with a special lighting system that recreates the sun in Japan. We walked the aisles, smelling the different leaves and flowers—the aromas were incredible. We visited the farm at the beginning of the citrus season, so most of their citrus—including beautiful little kumquats, yuzu, Buddha's hand and calamansi—was still unripe.

When we get their citrus fruit, the fruit usually goes straight to the bar, where it is infused, steeped and turned into syrups, shrubs and powders. We use everything, in multiple ways and multiple times; nothing goes to waste, and the last process is usually a dehydration of the "waste" that is transformed into a powder and used as a garnish. Our bartender loves an O'Citrus delivery day—the prep day gets longer, but the results are always worth it!

Canadian Sour

This cocktail was created after a hard and busy dinner service. On these occasions, a refreshing cocktail is often appreciated by the team, and our bar manager, Shannon Marshall, whipped this up. Balsam fir is his secret weapon in cocktails, and we had freshly made shrub from the most beautiful yuzu at O'Citrus (page 155). The team fell in love with it instantly and nicknamed it Perch Punch. When it made its way onto the menu, it became a top seller quickly.

Quince-infused whisky

6 quinces, stemmed, cored and roughly chopped
750 mL Pike Creek Whisky

Yuzu shrub

(131%) 197 g sugar
(2.5%) 3.8 g citric acid
(1%) 1.5 g malic acid
(100%) Zest and 150 g fresh juice from yuzu
(112%) 168 g apple cider vinegar
(75%) 113 g water

Balsam fir syrup

(464%) 232 g sugar
(660%) 330 g water
(8%) 4 g citric acid
(100%) 50 g dried balsam fir leaves

Citric acid solution

(708%) 170 g water
(100%) 24 g citric acid
(12.5%) 3 g malic acid

Canadian Sour

2 oz Quince-Infused Whisky (see here)
¾ oz Balsam Fir Syrup (see here)
¾ oz verjus
½ oz Yuzu Shrub (see here)
1 bar spoon Citric Acid Solution (see here)
1 egg white
4 dashes Angostura bitters

Quince-infused whisky Combine both ingredients in a lidded container. Set aside at room temperature to infuse for 3 weeks.

Strain, reserving the solids for Rabbit and Balsam Fir Sauce (page 70).

Yuzu shrub Note: This shrub is different from other shrub recipes in the book. As the zest releases very little liquid, I've added yuzu juice and water to compensate for its low yield.

In a lidded jar, combine sugar, citric acid, malic acid and yuzu zest. Screw on the lid, then shake to mix. Set aside at room temperature for 24 hours.

Add yuzu juice, vinegar and water. Stir to mix, then set aside at room temperature for another 24 hours.

Strain into a bottle, then refrigerate.

The shrub can be stored in the fridge for up to 3 months.

Balsam fir syrup In a medium saucepan, combine sugar, water and citric acid and cook over low heat until sugar has fully dissolved. Remove from heat, then stir in dried balsam fir. Steep for 30 minutes.

Strain through a fine-mesh strainer lined with a cheesecloth or oil filter. Bottle, then refrigerate.

The syrup can be stored in the fridge for up to 1 month.

Citric acid solution Heat water in a saucepan to a temperature of 80°C (175°F). Add both acids and stir until dissolved. Let cool.

The solution can be stored at room temperature or in the fridge for up to 3 months.

Canadian Sour Combine all ingredients except Angostura bitters in a cocktail shaker. Dry shake for 10–15 seconds. Add ice, then shake until very chilled. Double strain into a coupe glass, then top with Angostura bitters.

Field Trip

This cocktail was created from the scraps of our Rhubarb and Elderflower dish (page 148) and gorgeous first-of-the-season strawberries gifted from Rideau Pines Farm. As summer took hold, this incredibly refreshing, complex yet easy-to-drink beverage made perfect sense.

Strawberry and sage syrup

- (100%) 360 g strawberries, chopped and tops reserved
- (55%) 198 g sugar
- 1 bar spoon citric acid
- (111%) 400 g water
- (1.5%) 5.4 g sage leaves

Rhubarb and strawberry top shrub

- (100%) 400 g rhubarb stalks, chopped
- (17%) 68 g reserved strawberry tops from Strawberry and Sage Syrup (see here)
- (35%) 140 g sugar
- (117%) 468 g apple cider vinegar

Field Trip

- 1½ oz Fonseca Siroco White Port
- 1 oz Amaro Montenegro
- ¾ oz Rhubarb and Strawberry Top Shrub (see here)
- ½ oz Strawberry and Sage Syrup (see here)
- 2 oz club soda

Strawberry and sage syrup In a lidded container, combine strawberries, sugar and citric acid. Cover with the lid and shake to combine. Set aside to macerate at room temperature for 8 hours or overnight.

In a medium saucepan, combine the strawberry mixture and water and heat over low heat until sugar has dissolved. Remove from heat, then stir in sage. Set aside to steep for 20 minutes.

Strain through a fine-mesh strainer lined with a cheesecloth or oil filter, squeezing out any excess juice from strawberries. Bottle, then refrigerate.

The syrup can be stored in the fridge for up to 1 week.

Rhubarb and strawberry top shrub In a lidded jar, combine rhubarb, strawberry tops and sugar. Screw on the lid, then shake to mix. Set aside to macerate at room temperature for 24 hours.

Stir in vinegar. Set aside at room temperature for another 24 hours.

Refrigerate for 3 days to infuse.

Strain into a bottle, then refrigerate.

The shrub can be stored in the fridge for up to 3 months.

Field Trip Fill a cocktail shaker with all ingredients except club soda. Shake for 10–15 seconds. Add ice, then shake again until well chilled.

Add a Collins cube to a Collins glass. Strain the mixture into the glass, then top with soda and stir.

Follow the Leader

I once bought Moldavian balm seeds not knowing exactly what they were and gave them to Bower Farm (page 51) to grow for us. When we received the final product, I was surprised it had such a unique and vibrant flavour. We brought in a ton of it, and our bar manager, Shannon, got to work in adding it to a cocktail.

He had added a bunch of leftover corn cobs from a corn-and-mushroom course to whisky as an experiment. Adding the complexity of fermented koji water to it, he created this beautiful, stiff, cold-weather drink.

Corn cob–infused whisky

7 corn cobs, quartered
750 mL Suntory Toki Whisky

Moldavian balm honey syrup

(100%) 200 g honey
(50%) 100 g water
(20%) 40 g dried Moldavian balm leaves

Smoked salt solution

(100%) 80 g water
(25%) 20 g smoked sea salt

Follow the Leader

2 oz Corn Cob–Infused Whisky (see here)
¾ oz Moldavian Balm Honey Syrup (see here)
½ oz IZUMI Black Label Sake
½ oz Lacto-Koji Water (page 176)
½ oz verjus
2 bar spoons citric acid
2 drops Smoked Salt Solution (see here)

Corn cob–infused whisky Shave off any corn kernels from cobs. Combine corn cobs and whisky in a 2-litre jar or a jar large enough to fit both. Set aside at room temperature for 1–2 weeks.

Strain into a bottle.

The infused whisky can be stored in the fridge for up to 3 months.

Moldavian balm honey syrup Heat honey and water in a saucepan over low heat until combined. Remove from heat, then stir in Moldavian balm. Set aside to infuse at room temperature for 24 hours.

Strain into a bottle.

Leftover syrup can be stored in the fridge for up to 1 week.

Smoked salt solution Combine both ingredients in a saucepan and simmer until salt has dissolved. Set aside to cool. Transfer to a bottle.

Follow the Leader Fill a cocktail shaker with all ingredients. Shake for 10–15 seconds. Add ice, then shake again until well chilled. Strain into a rocks glass.

Garden Party

Our cedar-cured Asparagus and Lobster (page 100) creates an abundance of asparagus trimmings and peel. To eliminate food waste, we started making shrubs and infusing alcohol with them. This cocktail took quite a few attempts, but the final product met our expectations: a complex and refreshing beverage to start off a tasting menu and awaken the palate.

Asparagus gin

(100%) 750 mL Georgian Bay Gin
(115%) 863 g asparagus trim, peels and woody stems

Honey Prosecco syrup

(100%) 250 g flat Prosecco
(100%) 250 g honey

Garden Party

1½ oz Asparagus Gin (see here)
¼ oz Honey Prosecco Syrup (see here)
¼ oz Asparagus Shrub (page 176)
¼ oz Lillet Blanc
¼ oz verjus
2 drops Saline Solution (page 175)
2 oz Prosecco
3 dashes cucumber bitters

Asparagus gin Combine both ingredients in a lidded container and cover with the lid. Set aside to infuse at room temperature for 1–2 weeks.

Strain into a bottle.

Honey Prosecco syrup Combine both ingredients in a saucepan and heat over low heat until honey has dissolved. Set aside to cool. Transfer to a bottle.

Leftover syrup can be stored in the fridge for up to 1 week.

Garden Party In a cocktail shaker, combine all ingredients except Prosecco and bitters. Add ice, then shake for 10–15 seconds until chilled.

Strain into a coupe glass. Top with Prosecco and finish with cucumber bitters.

Lost in Migration

Our bar manager Shannon's favourite classic cocktail is a Jungle Bird, but most of its ingredients aren't grown in Canada.

One day, an abundance of fresh peaches were delivered to the restaurant, and my partner, Amanda, fermented a good portion of them. The combination of fermented peaches with nectarine juice, pineappleweed, sea buckthorn and rich duck fat reminded Shannon of a Jungle Bird.

While not a true Jungle Bird, this is a very Canadian version that adds a ton of fun to a similar profile.

Lacto-peach juice

- (100%) 1 kg ripe peaches, lightly cleaned
- (2%) 20 g salt

Duck fat rum

- (30%) 225 g duck fat
- (100%) 750 mL Flor de Caña Five-Year Rum

Pineappleweed syrup

- (100%) 100 g sugar
- (100%) 100 g water
- (25%) 25 g dried pineappleweed

Lost in Migration

- 2 oz Duck Fat Rum (see here)
- ½ oz Lacto-Peach Juice (see here)
- ½ oz nectarine juice
- ½ oz Campari
- ¼ oz Pineappleweed Syrup (see here)
- ¼ oz sea buckthorn verjus (the juice of unripe sea buckthorn berries)
- 4 dashes peach bitters

Lacto-peach juice Cut peaches in half, then remove stones. Cut each half into quarters. Combine peaches and salt in a bowl and mix well.

Transfer salted peaches to a 3-litre fermentation jar that's fitted with an airlock. Place a fermentation weight on top of the fruit so the fruit remains submerged in juices as it macerates. Seal the jar. Set aside to ferment at room temperature for 5 days but ferment to taste.

Strain the liquid into a container. Place peaches in a juicer and juice. Pour juice into the container. (The leftover peach solids can be dehydrated and made into a flavourful seasoning powder for use in Squab Liver Mousse Bunuelos [page 60].)

Duck fat rum Gently heat duck fat in a saucepan over low heat until liquified.

Combine duck fat and rum in a lidded container and cover with the lid. Gently shake, then set aside to infuse at room temperature overnight.

Put the mixture into the freezer and freeze for 12 hours, until the fat separates and solidifies. Strain through cheesecloth into a bottle. Approximate yield: 750 mL.

Leftover rum can be stored in the fridge for 1 month.

Pineappleweed syrup Combine sugar and water in a saucepan and heat over low heat until sugar has dissolved. Remove from heat, then stir in pineappleweed. Set aside to infuse at room temperature for 24 hours.

Strain into a bottle.

Leftover syrup can be stored in the fridge for up to 1 week.

Lost in Migration Combine all ingredients except peach bitters in a cocktail shaker. Add ice, then shake for 10–15 seconds until well chilled.

Double strain into a rocks glass with a king cube, then finish with peach bitters.

Saint Burden

We must have tested this cocktail twenty to thirty times. It was my pet project for a cocktail, the only one I ever made from start to finish (with a lot of discussion with Shannon). We love mirin at Perch, but there is no Canadian mirin and the more widely available options in Canada are low-quality, glucose-infused flavouring.

We developed a buckwheat mirin for several months before it began to taste of a refined crème de cacao–type liquor. It was incredible. The tests began, and I eventually finalized this recipe. For the first quarter of 2024, all proceeds from this cocktail were donated to the Burnt Chef Project, for which I'm a Canadian ambassador.

Buckwheat mirin

- (33%) 165 g toasted buckwheat
- (100%) 500 g Georgian Bay Vodka
- (33%) 165 g fresh Koji (page 175)

Saint Burden

- 1 oz Los Arango Tequila
- ¾ oz Buckwheat Mirin (see here)
- ½ oz Yellow Chartreuse
- ½ oz Rosewood Solera Mead
- 3 dashes orange bitters
- 3 drops Saline Solution (page 175)
- 1 bar spoon simple syrup

Buckwheat mirin Cook buckwheat according to package instructions.

Combine all ingredients in a high-powered blender and blend until smooth. Transfer to a bottle and cover with an airtight lid. Set aside at room temperature for 5 months.

Strain into another bottle.

Leftover mirin can be stored in the fridge for 1 month.

Saint Burden Combine all ingredients in a mixing glass. Fill with ice, then stir for 15–20 seconds. Strain into a chilled Nick & Nora glass.

Snap Decision

This is another cocktail created from food waste. Pea pods are a huge waste in restaurants, usually going straight into the garbage. We sat down and devised a plan for them. My partner, Amanda, concocted a shrub, a schnapps and a syrup with them (we had a lot!), while our bar manager, Shannon, used those new ingredients to create a cocktail that perfectly reflected our ethos.

Snap pea schnapps

- (53%) 265 g snap pea pods, roughly chopped
- (21%) 105 g sugar
- (100%) 500 g Georgian Bay Vodka

Snap pea syrup

- (100%) 250 g snap pea pods, roughly chopped
- (100%) 250 g sugar
- (50%) 125 g boiling water

Snap Decision

- 1¾ oz Snap Pea Schnapps (see here)
- ½ oz Snap Pea Shrub (page 177)
- ¼ oz Snap Pea Syrup (see here)
- ¼ oz St-Germain
- ¼ oz verjus
- 1 egg white
- 2 drops Saline Solution (page 175)
- 4 dashes elderflower bitters

Snap pea schnapps Combine pea pods and sugar in a 1-litre jar with a lid. Screw on the lid, then shake to combine. Set aside to macerate at room temperature for 24 hours.

Stir in vodka. Set aside at room temperature for 1 month to infuse.

Strain into a bottle.

Leftover schnapps can be stored in the fridge for 1 month.

Snap pea syrup Combine pea pods and sugar in a 1-litre heatproof jar with a lid. Screw on the lid, then shake to mix. Set aside to macerate at room temperature for 48 hours, stirring occasionally.

Pour in boiling water and mix to dissolve any remaining sugar. Strain into a bottle.

Leftover syrup can be stored in the fridge for up to 1 week.

Snap Decision In a cocktail shaker, combine all ingredients except elderflower bitters. Dry shake for 15–20 seconds. Add ice, then shake until well chilled.

Double strain into a coupe glass, then top with elderflower bitters.

Street Magician

Because espresso grounds are the inevitable by-product of our coffee program, we do what we can to reduce waste. So we combine spent espresso grounds and fryer oil (along with potassium hydroxide, vegetable glycerin and citric acid) to make an all-natural hand soap for use in our washrooms. Shannon also does an incredible job of incorporating them into our bar program. "Oh, dang, buddy!" were my first words when I tasted this creation, which reminded me of a complex Manhattan. As far as I'm concerned, it's an instant classic.

Spent coffee syrup

- (100%) 60 g dehydrated spent coffee grounds
- (166%) 100 g sugar
- (166%) 100 g brown sugar
- (568%) 341 g water

Spent coffee syrup Combine all ingredients in a saucepan and heat over medium heat until both sugars have dissolved. Remove from heat, then set aside to steep for 20 minutes.

Strain through a fine-mesh strainer lined with a coffee filter into a bottle and refrigerate.

Leftover syrup can be stored in the fridge for up to 1 week.

Street Magician

- 1¼ oz Pike Creek Whisky
- ½ oz Cynar
- ½ oz Amaro Nonino Quintessentia®
- ½ oz Spent Coffee Syrup (see here)
- 1 bar spoon Yellow Chartreuse
- 2 dashes Angostura bitters
- 2 dashes orange bitters

Street Magician Combine all ingredients in a mixing glass. Add ice, then stir for 15–20 seconds. Strain into a chilled Nick & Nora glass.

essentials

Saline Solution

(100%) 80 g water at 80°C (175°F)
(25%) 20 g sea salt

Combine both ingredients in a bowl.
Stir until salt is completely dissolved.

Seaweed Water

(100%) 200 g water
(1%) 2 g bull kelp
(1%) 2 g dulse
(1%) 2 g sugar kelp

Combine all ingredients in a bowl. Refrigerate overnight. Strain.

Koji

While I use a more standardized temperature that works well across a variety of fermented products, you can influence the end product through heat. Higher temperatures will impact different enzyme behaviours and increase protease activity, enhancing umami in products like miso. Cooler temperatures slow down the fermentation process, which can result in a more gradual breakdown of starches and sugars. This can be beneficial for products like amazake (a sweet, fermented rice drink), where a sweeter profile is desirable.

(100%) 750 g long-grain or sushi rice
(0.1%) 0.75 g *Aspergillus oryzae* spores
(0.75%) 5.6 g rice flour

Rinse rice until the water runs clear. Place rice in a bowl, add water, and soak for 12–24 hours.

Prepare a steaming basket by bringing the water to a simmer. Place rice in the steaming basket and steam for about 45 minutes. Spread rice on a tray and cool as quickly as possible while fanning rice until its temperature reaches 25°C–34°C (77°F–93°F).

Line a cedar tray or hotel pan with a linen napkin and spread rice in the pan.

In a bowl, mix *Aspergillus oryzae* spores and rice flour, then dust half of the mixture over rice. Gently mix rice, then dust the remaining spore mixture on top.

Place the tray in a proofer set to 32°C (90°F), with a tray of water to maintain humidity (we use the Brod & Taylor Proofer), and incubate. After 18 hours, gently mix rice and create little mounds in rows so the koji doesn't overheat (it creates its own heat as it grows). Check rice every 6 hours for 30–48 hours, giving it a slight mix and creating small mounds if the internal temperature becomes too warm. The koji is ready when it has a sweet aroma and a white, fuzzy appearance. If it begins to turn green, remove the tray from the proofer to halt the growth of the spores. Remove any green spots from the koji before using.

For dried koji, remove the koji from the proofer and break it up into individual pieces. Place in a dehydrator set at 40°C (105°F) till completely dried.

You can adjust the incubation temperature to favour the production of different enzymes. If you wish to explore the world of koji further, many excellent books and websites are available.

Lacto-Koji Water

- (100%) 250 g water
- (50%) 125 g fresh Koji (page 175)
- (3%) 8 g non-iodized salt

Combine all ingredients in a high-powered blender and blend until smooth.

Pour the mixture into a fermentation jar that's fitted with an airlock, then press plastic wrap onto the surface of the liquid. Seal the jar. Set aside at room temperature for 5 days.

Strain through cheesecloth into a container.

Leftover lacto-koji water can be stored in the fridge for 5 days or the freezer for 3 months.

Shio Koji

- (100%) 100 g Koji (page 175)
- (100%) 100 g water
- (10%) 10 g salt

Combine all ingredients in a high-powered blender and blitz until smooth. Pour the mixture into a jar and set aside at room temperature for 5 days.

Asparagus Shrub

- (100%) 225 g asparagus trim, peels and woody stems
- (30%) 68 g sugar
- (100%) 225 g white wine vinegar

Combine asparagus and sugar in a lidded container and cover with the lid. Shake to mix. Set aside to macerate at room temperature for 24 hours.

Stir in vinegar. Set aside at room temperature for another 24 hours.

Refrigerate for 2 days to infuse.

Strain the liquid into a bottle.

Leftover shrub can be stored in the fridge for 3 weeks.

Carrot Top Shrub

- (100%) 200 g carrot tops, chopped
- (34%) 68 g sugar
- (100%) 200 g white wine vinegar

Mix carrot tops with sugar in a lidded container. Cover with the lid and set aside at room temperature for 24 hours.

Refrigerate for another 24 hours.

Add vinegar, then refrigerate for 3 days.

Strain through a fine-mesh strainer. Pour shrub into a mister bottle.

Leftover shrub can be stored in the fridge for 3 weeks.

Kohlrabi Shrub

The kohlrabi pulp is from the koji-fermented kohlrabi juice in Ramp Spaghettini (page 58). White wine vinegar is also made from our wine program (so is our red wine vinegar), using wine that is slightly past its prime as a beverage.

- (100%) 250 g kohlrabi pulp
- (30%) 75 g sugar
- (100%) 250 g white wine vinegar

Combine kohlrabi pulp and sugar in a lidded container and cover with the lid. Shake to mix, then set aside to macerate at room temperature for 24 hours.

Stir in vinegar. Set aside to infuse at room temperature for 24 hours.

Refrigerate for 2 days to infuse.

Strain into a container with a lid.

Leftover shrub can be stored in the fridge for 3 weeks.

Snap Pea Shrub

- (100%) 250 g snap pea pods, roughly chopped
- (45%) 113 g sugar
- (100%) 250 g white wine vinegar

Combine pea pods and sugar in a lidded container and cover with the lid. Shake to mix, then set aside to macerate at room temperature for 24 hours.

Stir in vinegar. Set aside to infuse at room temperature for 24 hours.

Refrigerate for 2 days to infuse.

Strain into a bottle.

Leftover shrub can be stored in the fridge for 3 weeks.

Tomato Shrub

- (100%) 400 g tomato, chopped
- (34%) 136 g sugar
- (100%) 400 g rice wine vinegar

Mix tomato and sugar in a lidded container. Cover with the lid and set aside at room temperature for 24 hours.

Refrigerate for another 24 hours.

Stir in vinegar, then set aside at room temperature for 24 hours.

Transfer shrub to the fridge and refrigerate for 72 hours.

Strain through a fine-mesh strainer.

Leftover shrub can be stored in the fridge for 3 weeks

Garum

(100%) 1 kg meat with minimal fat, fat trimmed
(80%) 800 g water
(24%) 240 g salt or sea salt
(20%) 200 g Koji (page 175)

Note: Make sure to have a very clean and sterilized fermentation vessel.

Grind meat in a meat grinder set with a small die.

Combine all ingredients in a clean bowl. Using an immersion blender, emulsify the mixture. Pour the mixture into a fermentation vessel, place a piece of plastic wrap on the surface of the liquid and seal the vessel. Set aside at 60°C (140°F) for 30 days.

Once a week, skim the surface to remove any fat and stir the mixture, replacing the plastic wrap each time.

After 30 days, strain garum through a fine-mesh strainer, reserving the solids. If you find the liquid is too intense, dilute it with water and bring the total weight of the liquid to ~800 g. Reserve the liquid in an airtight container in the fridge for up to 1 month or the freezer for much longer.

Place the solids in a dehydrator set at 55°C (131°F) until completely dried. Blend in a blender to form a fine powder. Use garum as a seasoning or umami punch in broths.

Resources

Below is a list of companies that, at the time of print, are dedicated to supporting local farming and sustainable practices—values that align with our own commitment to environmental responsibility. These organizations and initiatives play a crucial role in promoting sustainable agriculture, reducing environmental impact and fostering a stronger, more resilient local food system. We're proud to support their efforts and share these resources with you.

1847 Stone Milling (flour, grains)
1847.ca

Acadian Sturgeon and Caviar (sturgeon, caviar)
Acadian-sturgeon.com

Affinity Fish (fish)
Affinityfish.com

The Barking Bee Company (honey)
Thebarkingbeecompany.ca

Bower Farm (produce)
Bowerfarm.ca

Bush Berry (foraged teas)
Bushberry.ca

Dulse Adventure (dulse seaweed)
Dulseadventure.com

Enright Cattle Co. (beef)
Enrightcattlecompany.com

Featherstone Estate Winery (verjus)
Featherstonewinery.ca

Ferme Rêveuse (eggs, chicken)
Ferme-reveuse.ca

Foggy Shoals Fish Co. (fish, shellfish)
Foggyshoals.com

Forager Bee (locally foraged ingredients and honey)
Foragerbee.square.site

Forbes Wild Foods (wild Canadian ingredients, such as birch)
Wildfoods.ca

Golden Eagle Black Cod (black cod)
Geblackcod.com

Heart City Farm (produce, including microgreens)
Heartcity.farm

Hedgerow Orchard (sea buckthorn)
Hedgeroworchard.ca

IZUMI (sake)
Izumibrewery.com

Juniper Farm (produce)
Juniperfarm.ca

Kamosu (miso)
Kamosumiso.com

La Brasserie San-Ô (koji spores)
Labrasseriesan-o.ca

Les Jardiniers du chef (edible flowers)
Jardiniersduchef.com

Little Farm Cart (produce, flowers)
Littlefarmcart.com

Lulo Coffee (coffee, cascara)
Lulocoffee.ca

Mariposa Farm (poultry, meat)
Mariposa-duck.on.ca

O'Citrus (citrus)
No website

Old Habits Fermentation Co. (fish sauce)
Oldhabitsfermentationco.com

The Olive Farm (olive oil)
Theolivefarm.ca

Organic Ocean (fish, seafood)
Organicocean.com

Pacific Wild Pick (wild West Coast ingredients)
Pacificwildpick.com

Peconic Escargot (escargots)
Peconicescargot.com

Raon Kitchen (gochujang)
Raonkitchen.com

Rideau Pines Farm (produce)
Rideaupinesfarm.com

Rosewood Wines (wine, mead)
Rosewoodwine.com

Rutabaga Ranch (produce)
Rutabaga-ranch.com

Signé Caméline (camelina oil)
Signecameline.com

Stream Water (water)
Streamwater.ca

Terramor Farm (produce)
Terramorfarm.com

Trillium Meadows (red deer, venison, red wattle pork)
Trilliummeadows.ca

Vancouver Island Sea Salt (salt)
Canadianseasalt.com

Venturi-Schulze Vineyards (balsamic vinegar)
Venturischulze.com

Westcott Vineyards (verjus)
Westcottvineyards.com

Metric Conversion Chart

Liquid measures (for alcohol)

Imperial or U.S.		Metric
½ fl oz	→	15 mL
1 fl oz	→	30 mL
2 fl oz	→	60 mL
3 fl oz	→	90 mL
4 fl oz	→	120 mL

Weight

Imperial or U.S.		Metric
½ oz	→	15 g
1 oz	→	30 g
2 oz	→	60 g
3 oz	→	85 g
4 oz (¼ lb)	→	115 g
5 oz	→	140 g
6 oz	→	170 g
7 oz	→	200 g
8 oz (½ lb)	→	225 g
9 oz	→	255 g
10 oz	→	285 g
11 oz	→	310 g
12 oz (¾ lb)	→	340 g
13 oz	→	370 g
14 oz	→	400 g
15 oz	→	425 g
16 oz (1 lb)	→	450 g
1¼ lbs	→	570 g
1½ lbs	→	675 g
2 lbs	→	900 g
3 lbs	→	1.4 kg
4 lbs	→	1.8 kg
5 lbs	→	2.3 kg
6 lbs	→	2.7 kg

Cans and jars

Imperial or U.S.		Metric
6 oz	→	170 mL
14 oz	→	398 mL
19 oz	→	540 mL
28 oz	→	796 mL

Baking pans

Imperial or U.S.		Metric
5- × 9-inch loaf pan	→	2 L loaf pan
9- × 13-inch cake pan	→	4 L cake pan
11- × 17-inch sheet	→	30- × 45-cm baking baking sheet

Linear

Imperial or U.S.		Metric
1/32 inch	→	1 mm
1/24 inch	→	1.5 mm
1/16 inch	→	2 mm
⅛ inch	→	3 mm
¼ inch	→	5 or 6 mm
½ inch	→	1 cm or 12 mm
¾ inch	→	2 cm
1 inch	→	2.5 cm
1¼ inches	→	3 cm
1½ inches	→	3.5 cm
1¾ inches	→	4.5 cm
2 inches	→	5 cm
2½ inches	→	6 or 6.5 cm
2¾ inches	→	7 cm
3 inches	→	7.5 cm
3¼ inches	→	8 cm
4 inches	→	10 cm
5 inches	→	12.5 cm
6 inches	→	15 cm
7 inches	→	18 cm
10 inches	→	25 cm
12 inches (1 foot)	→	30 cm
13 inches	→	33 cm
16 inches	→	41 cm
18 inches	→	46 cm
24 inches (2 feet)	→	60 cm
28 inches	→	70 cm
30 inches	→	75 cm
6 feet	→	1.8 m

Temperature

(For oven temperatures, see chart below)

Imperial or U.S.		Metric
75°F	→	24°C
77°F	→	25°C
90°F	→	32°C
93°F	→	34°C
105°F	→	40°C
113°F	→	45°C
120°F	→	49°C
122°F	→	50°C
125°F	→	52°C
130°F	→	54°C
131°F	→	55°C
136°F	→	58°C
140°F	→	60°C
147°F	→	64°C
149°F	→	65°C
150°F	→	66°C
155°F	→	68°C
158°F	→	70°C
160°F	→	71°C
165°F	→	74°C
170°F	→	77°C
174°F	→	79°C
175°F	→	80°C
180°F	→	82°C
185°F	→	85°C
190°F	→	88°C
200°F	→	93°C
203°F	→	95°C
212°F	→	100°C
230°F	→	110°C
233°F	→	112°C
240°F	→	115°C or 116°C
248°F	→	120°C
250°F	→	121°C
275°F	→	135°C
300°F	→	149°C
325°F	→	163°C
347°F	→	175°C
350°F	→	177°C
360°F	→	182°C
375°F	→	191°C
401°F	→	205°C

Oven temperature

Imperial or U.S.		Metric
140°F	→	60°C
200°F or 203°F	→	95°C
210°F	→	99°C
221°F	→	105°C
250°F	→	120°C
275°F	→	135°C
300°F	→	148°C or 150°C
325°F	→	160°C
347°F	→	175°C
350°F	→	177°C or 180°C
375°F	→	190°C
400°F	→	200°C
401°F	→	205°C
419°F	→	215°C
424°F	→	218°C
425°F	→	220°C
450°F	→	230°C
500°F	→	260°C
550°F	→	290°C

Acknowledgements

A ridiculous number of people need to be acknowledged not only for helping create this book or Perch but also for helping me through my life by continually pushing me to take the next step.

Thank you to my team. All staff, past and present, have been integral to the success of Perch. Since day one, I've always felt so lucky to have and appreciative for this amazing team—you're all rock stars.

I would like to express my deepest and most sincere gratitude to the photography team, particularly Sarah Farmer of Gumption Studio for her incredible support and artistry in capturing the stunning photographs for this cookbook. Sarah's talent, attention to detail and dedication have truly brought each recipe to life in the most beautiful way. Thank you to Nick Ghattas of Midnight Hour Studios for allowing us to use his studio for all our food photography. A good amount of the plateware used for the recipe photography was gifted by Will Mann of Brewmaster Ceramics, Brad Ruff of Rough Seas Woodworks and Nina Marchewka. Thank you for the exceptional pieces, which made the food come to life!

A heartfelt thank you to my parents, Michel Lagarde and Michelle Champagne, and their partners, Lisa Cardinal and Darren Thatcher, for always being there with unwavering support. I am especially grateful to my grandparents Laurette and Paul Champagne, for instilling in me the work ethic that has shaped my career, and to my Baba, Marguerite Bodnar, whose introduction to the flavours that defined my palate has been a lasting influence.

I am deeply grateful to Sandra MacInnis and Robin Duetta, who have been pillars of strength and unwavering support through both the highs and lows of owning a restaurant. Bridget Sullivan and Jon Thibert were essential in opening Perch, dedicating countless hours to help renovate and shape the space into what it is today.

So many others have contributed to this book in ways big and small—if you're currently in my life or once were and we haven't spoken in a while, know that I appreciate you more than words can express. I truly never would have gotten here without each of you.

Above all, my heartfelt thanks go to Amanda MacIntosh, who has been by my side every step of the way. From guiding me through every major decision to offering constant support, you have been my greatest ally and the driving force behind this journey. Thank you, Amanda, for everything.

Index

Page numbers in italics refer to photos.

Chef Justin Champagne-Lagarde has made a significant mark on the Ottawa food scene with his acclaimed restaurant, Perch, which has impressed with its culinary excellence. Critics and diners alike have praised its innovative tasting menus, which are designed to showcase the talents of his teams and highlight his commitment to locally sourced ingredients, ethical farming practices and sustainability. As well, the restaurant has gained a reputation for its exquisite dishes and impeccable service. Perch was recognized as one of the best new restaurants in Canada by *enRoute* in 2022 and featured in *Canada's 100 Best* in 2023.

As a proud member of the local and professional community, Justin is a Canadian ambassador for the Burnt Chef Project and involved in many community-led ventures and undertakings, such as the annual Wild Path Dinner at Anupaya (page 20), Harvest, Feast of Fields and Raw:almond. He actively collaborates with top chefs in Canada such as Julian Bentivegna (Ten Restaurant), Mandel Hitzer (deer + almond) and Zach Keeshig (Naagan), with more collaborations in the works.

Perch @perchottawa
Justin @champagne.chef

Sarah Farmer, founder of Gumption Studio, is a Canadian photographer and food stylist whose work is deeply rooted in her culinary background. A former fine dining chef and pastry chef, Sarah brings a unique understanding of food's textures, colours and narratives to her photography. She specializes in creating bold, vibrant and evocative images that capture the essence of her clients' vision.

Her work has been widely recognized and featured in publications such as *Canada's 100 Best*, *enRoute*, *Canadian Geographic*, *re:Porter*, *MENU*, *Ottawa Magazine*, *LUXE Ottawa* and *Edible Ottawa*, as well as on *Top Chef Canada*. Sarah was also featured on *My Story, My Lens* on Fibe TV1, where she shared her journey from chef to photographer.

Sarah remains closely connected to her culinary roots through impactful projects like *The Last Service*, a national photo series that aimed to bring attention to challenges and accomplishments of the food and beverage industry. She is also a co-founder of Anupaya's annual Wild Path Dinner, an event that celebrates the intersection of food, community and nature (page 20).